The WAR
We Almost
LOST

How We Came Close To Losing World War II

ARTHUR A. EDWARDS
Ex Lieutenant, USNR

Inks and Bindings
888-290-5218
www.inksandbindings.com
orders@inksandbindings.com

Contents

Foreword

Many books have been written about World War II by historians and people who had axes to grind and points to make. People who hated President Franklin Roosevelt have been vocal in their criticism of him, his administration and our military's preparations for war under his leadership. Stories have been told about our being "asleep at the switch," when we were attacked by Japan, by people who were most critical of President Roosevelt for trying to prepare us for the upcoming war.

The most ridiculous argument is the one claiming that the President knew about the upcoming Japanese attack on Pearl Harbor in advance. This fable persists that he did not warn the sailors and soldiers in advance because he wanted to enter the war to protect his friend Winston Churchill. The argument goes that we had cracked the secret Japanese code and therefore must have intercepted a transmission that their fleet was on its way.

All of this is in spite of the fact that the Japanese records show that no transmission, coded or otherwise, was ever sent by the Japanese government stating that the Imperial Navy intended to attack Pearl Harbor on December 7th. This is confirmed by the fact that even their ally, Adolph Hitler was surprised by the attack. But people who postulate these and other wild theories are not confused by facts.

Having lived through the war and the decade leading up to it, I have often thought that a book needed to be written clarifying our preparations prior to Pearl Harbor. Such a book must include the lack of readiness of our military and actions of politicians that had a profound effect on our prewar condition and inability to respond to the

Axis attacks. It is not a tale that Americans should be proud of, but we recovered in time and won the greatest victory of all times. Victory was not always certain however, and were it not for a few serious blunders by our enemies, the outcome might well have been very different.

This book is written to clarify events in the thirties and forties emphasizing those that have been mischaracterized or overlooked by people who were not there. The author lived through it all, listened to the events on the radio at his father's knee before his dad joined the Navy. Art heard them as they unfolded, talked to returning servicemen, studied the events while training to be a naval officer and has read many books on the subject since.

Although this book is based on these experiences, the conclusions reached are the authors entirely. He hopes to create enough interest in the subject that readers will continue the search for their own truths without being misled by preconceptions.

The decade between 1932 and 1942 was very important and critical to our understanding of our preparations for the war. The events that led to the war need to be told as accurately as we know them whether you liked President Roosevelt or not. It is hoped that the reader will discard his or her preconceptions and dig into this book with an open mind.

Author's Previous Publications

War is Hell -A novel about fighting in the Burma jungle during WW II and the effects it has on the men and women who fought it. Robertson Publishing, Fremont California

A Hero's Life – A novel about an aerospace engineer who was a WII hero who finds himself in a bind trying to identify the cause of multiple crashes of his company's prize fighter plane. Robertson Publishing, Fremont, California

The Journey to Hangtown Haven – A true story about a small town's attempt to solve its homeless problem and the community's negative response to building a shelter for its homeless citizens. Robertson Publishing. Fremont, California.

Definitions

Since many readers were not yet born when WW II started, the following terms that appear in the book are defined here for clarification.

Allies – The nations that joined together to fight the Axis nations including; The United States, Great Britain, China, The Soviet Union, Canada, Australia, New Zealand and South Africa.

Axis. The nations that joined together to conquer the world including; Germany, Japan, Austria (Hitler was born in Austria), Italy (until 1943), plus other countries that supported the Axis but did not join them; Spain (Spain provided some troops to the German army at Stalingrad) and Finland ((more anti Soviet than pro German). Romania and Hungary were not technically a member of the axis group, but both provided troops to fight alongside of the German army.

Pro Axis Neutral Countries – Turkey, Portugal, Ireland, Argentina, Uruguay

Actual Neutral countries – Sweden and Switzerland

Countries that were over run and conquered by Axis troops – Holland, France, Poland, Czechoslovakia, Yugoslavia, Greece, Belgium, Denmark, Norway, Parts of China, Indonesia, Burma, Philippines and Mongolia.

Wehrmacht – The German army

Luftwaffe – The German air force

Messerschmitt – The German company the made the **Luftwaffe's** ME-109 (sometimes known as the bf-109) fighter plan

Spitfire – The Royal Air Force's fighter plane made by Supermarine in England.

IJN – Imperial Japanese Navy

Dedication

This book is dedicated to my wife Shirly, who pulled this manuscript out of my desk one day and asked, "Why don't you publish this, Honey?" So here it is.

I owe a deep sense of gratitude and thanks to my computer repair friend Jason Primicerio, without whose help and advice this book would not have been possible.

My daughter, Diana was the author in our family and encouraged me to write until she died of a heart attack in 2012 at the age of fifty just after she was awarded her MBA at Stanford. I miss her very much and wish I could share this book with her. Maybe she can read it where she is now. Who knows?

My friends and neighbors Betsy Kerr and her husband, LCDR Dick Kerr, USNR retired, who read my original manuscript and made valuable suggestions

CHAPTER ONE

The Great Depression

Very few people alive today can imagine how serious the Hoover depression of the late twenties and thirties was to every country in the world. It hit the U. S. hard, but it probably hit Germany the hardest. Before we consider the effect of the depression on Germany, we must talk about the end of World War I and how the armistice affected Germany and its attitude toward the world.

Unfortunately, the foundation of World War II and the rise of Hitler can be found in the surrender of the Kaiser to the Allies in November of 1918. Actually, the Union Army's General William Sherman predicted it in 1864 when he stated famously that a war would never end until the civilians of the losing country felt the "hell" of war for themselves. Germany in 1918 had not been decimated or destroyed, as it would be in 1945. The Kaiser recognized that his troops had been defeated and his civilian population would be next, so he negotiated a peace that kept his population from experiencing the "hell" of war.

One would think that this was a good thing for the German population, but it turned out to be just the opposite. The question that faced the German civilians was, "Why did we lose? Nothing bad happened to us." Unfortunately, this was the foundation for the rise of Hitler in the late 1920's. He encouraged the people's anger against the Geneva Convention and the German depression to propel him into the chancellorship in 1933.

The world, including the United States, was unable to see the anger in the German population and predict its consequences on the rest of the world. A few, including Winston Churchill and Franklin Roosevelt, had the foresight to see it but they were almost alone in their respective countries in recognizing the war threats from Japan and Germany.

The Depression

It is beyond the scope of this book to dwell on the rise of Hitler and his effect on Germany. It is interesting to note for history that he and President Roosevelt became leaders of their respective countries in the same year, 1933. As Hitler rose in prominence during the 1930's, we must look at the effect that he had on American citizens. Unfortunately, there were many Americans, at least a large minority, who fell under Hitler's spell thousands of miles away from Germany. Most came from the following groups:

German Immigrants

As of the mid 1930's, Germany had provided more immigrants to the United States than had any other country. This may sound strange to those Americans who are now terrified of the influx of Latin Americans crossing our southern border. Thousands of German

Americans or children of German Americans looked back across the Atlantic and saw a new government that reflected some of their hopes, fears, prejudices and beliefs. Germany was not at war with the U. S. in the 1930's so there was nothing wrong in the eyes of many Americans with supporting Hitler and his attempts to eradicate Jews and other "undesirables" in Europe. Many ex -Germans in the U. S. were supporters of Nazi Germany before the war.

Irish

Many American supporters of Hitler were more against England than they were for Hitler. Such was the case with many Irish-American Immigrants. The Irish/English conflict goes back several hundred years and will not be discussed here. Suffice to say that there existed considerable animosity toward England from Irish immigrants in the U.S. during the 1930's. Joseph Kennedy was an excellent example of this.

Adolph Hitler

There was a story, never fully verified, of Irish dock workers planting bombs in cargo ships headed for England before we entered the war. These bombs blew up in the middle of the Atlantic sinking our ship in which they were planted. Obviously, it was hard to prove but the story goes that it was the Mafia that finally ended the practice. Whether it was a true story or not, there is no doubt that many Irish Americans supported Hitler before Pearl Harbor.

Scandinavian Countries

Some immigrants from Norway, Denmark, Sweden and Finland (not technically Scandinavian) were fascinated with Hitler and thought and that he was the answer to Germany's problems. Denmark and Norway are located nearby and socially close to Germany, while both Sweden and Finland supported Germany with needed supplies during the war. Sweden was technically neutral but provided ball bearings and steel to the German war effort. That support was often based on hundred year old resentment against the British. Some resentment is harder to get over than others.

The prime example of this attitude was seen in Charles Lindberg, an American aviation hero of Swedish parents. He toured the country in the 30's and early 40's preaching that we should be supporting Germany during the war and not England. When Germany declared war on the United States he tried to enlist as a pilot in the Army Air Corps but was prohibited from doing so by President Roosevelt. Lindberg eventually went to work for Lockheed and contributed to the war effort by leading squadrons of new P-38's across the Pacific into the war zone. In fact, he has the distinction of being the only American civilian to have shot down two enemy planes in combat. He did this over Guadalcanal. However, Roosevelt never forgave Lindberg for his activities in support of the Nazis before the war.

Other Countries

All of the countries in Europe were divided into three camps and their immigrants in the U.S. often reflected the attitudes of their home countries. The first group was made up of allies who would end up fighting Hitler: Great Britain, France, Holland, Belgium, Denmark, Poland Checkoslovakia, Norway, Greece and Serbia. The second group was made up of countries that actively supported Germany, although the Wehrmacht invaded some: Italy, Spain, Hungary, Austria, Romania, Croatia, Finland and the Soviet Union early in the war. The third group consisted of countries that were ostensibly neutral but that were basically supporting Germany: Ireland, Portugal, Turkey and Switzerland. (Switzerland was the only country in Europe that was actually neutral). In the Americas both Argentina and Uruguay were supporters of German aggression. Although France was a member of the Allied team, many individual Frenchmen and women supported Germany, particularly in rounding up Jews.

Roman Catholics

The attitude of the Holy Father before and during the war was hard to identify because neither Poe Pius XI nor Pope Pius XII ever officially stated their position one way or the other. There is evidence however that they secretly supported Hitler both in his elimination of the Jews and in Germany's fight against Protestant England. One proof of this is the existence of the American Catholic priest, Father Coughlin and his weekly radio program from New York City during the 30's.

Many people who listened to Father Coughlin commented that they couldn't tell his views from those of Hitler himself. Before you complain that it was only a priest giving his personal views it is a fact that no priest then or now could expound his extremist views on radio or television without the approval of his bishop, his archbishop, his cardinal and the pope. The popes were also known to have lived in Germany before becoming pope and both seemed to be in complete harmony with the new German government. There is considerable evidence that they fully supported Hitler's rise to power both financially and politically. In fairness to the popes, it is well known that Hitler agreed not to harass the Catholic Church if it stayed out of his hair. It is also well known that many individual priests worked against Hitler in Germany and occupied countries throughout Europe during the war.

Hitler Meeting with The Cardinal

People who support Pope Pius XII claim that there was nothing he could have done to stop Hitler at any time during the war. This is just not true. The pope could have slapped an interdiction on Germany which would probably have had a huge effect. Pope Innocent III did just that to Fredrick II and the Holy Roman Empire in the early thirteenth century and it had its intended effect.

The purpose of an ecclesiastical interdict is to deny everyone in a country the catholic sacraments such as marriage, baptism, confirmation, the Eucharist, penance and ordination. The people of The Holy Roman Empire were so overwhelmed by the interdict in the thirteenth century that they demanded that Fredrick accept the pope's demands and end it.

Father Coughlin

Frederick finally went crawling to the pope begging him to lift the interdict. Pope Pius XII could have done the same thing to Hitler when he realized that millions of Jews were being exterminated, but he did nothing. An interdict may or may not have had the desired effect on Hitler, but at least it would have shown that the pope was on the right side of history even if it had failed.

It is said that the only comment Pope Pius XII made about the war was to ask American General Mark Clark not to house "negroes" in the city when his Allied troops occupied Rome in 1944. Many American Catholics took their cue from Rome and were against preparing for war with Germany during the 30's.

World War I Survivors

Many Americans remembered the bloody conflict of World War I and did not want America to be involved in any war again. Many veterans of the Great War were still alive in the 30's, and many who had relatives who were veterans were not able to support preparations for another bloody conflict. That attitude was certainly understandable. Many WW I survivors had been subjected to gas attacks and many were "shell shocked." Very few veterans of the Great War were anxious to fight again.

Conservative Politicians Versus the President

Politics and politicians were not much different in the 30's than they are today excepting for one major characteristic. Although the Democratic Party is still the home for progressive thought, there was a large segment of the party who were hidebound conservatives before the war. To understand this phenomenon fully we need to look back at our Civil War.

The Democratic Party was based on support for the Confederacy before, during and after the Civil War era. Its members were typically white men who were more conservative than liberal and always voted for the Democrat running for office when it all changed in the mid 1960's . The shifting of alliances during the 60's will not be discussed here, but the election and reelection of President Roosevelt was largely due to the support of southern white men and women based on their refusal to vote for Lincoln's Republican party. Southern white men were typically anti-black and anti-immigration while their extreme wing, the Ku Klux Klan, was anti-Jewish and anti-Catholic as well. Although President Roosevelt was none of these, many who were had voted for the Democratic ticket during the 30's out of habit.

President Roosevelt was the consummate politician and knew well the precarious balance of northern liberals and southern conservatives that had voted him into office and would keep him there for four terms. His wife, Eleanor, probably the greatest woman of the twentieth century, pulled him into the progressive wing of his party. However, the president knew that he would lose considerable votes if he angered the Southern Democratic wing of his party. It was the liberal wing of his party that supported his efforts to prepare America for war, while his conservative supporters in the South objected to the cost of war preparation and the resulting need to raise taxes, a position that we see today in the Republican Party.

President Roosevelt had served as Assistant Secretary of The Navy in President Wilson's cabinet during WW I and had a deep affection for the navy. This affection carried well into the 1930's and turned out to be critical in the choices he made during his first two terms in office. He recognized quite clearly that the next war would be fought at sea as well as on land and began to build up our navy early in his tenure, much to the disgust of the conservatives and special interests mentioned earlier.

So, in summary, it is obvious that when you add up the people listed in previous paragraphs, there were a large number of Americans who were opposed to the President's efforts to build up the defenses of the country. The excuse used by members of the groups was that Hitler had warned every country in Europe that he would take the arming of neighboring countries personally and consider preparations to defend themselves as a threat to Germany's security.

President Roosevelt had his hands full with our depression and could only get something done through subterfuge and secrecy. In a democracy that was not easy.

Newspaper Headlines in 1932

It was known at the time that he would funnel money intended for dams and other civilian projects into building ships for the Navy. When confronted with this obviously illegal maneuver he would just shrug his shoulders and say, "It's better to ask for forgiveness than for permission." Many of our obsolete ships were replaced with modern vessels that were able to stand up to the Japanese fleet during the 40's because of President Roosevelt's "illegal" maneuvering.

Benito Mussolini

CHAPTER TWO

The Axis Dreams Of World Domination

J apan had long planned to extend its influence beyond its tranquil shores and into Asia. As early as the end of the nineteenth century, Japan contracted with Great Britain's Royal Navy to learn how to build warships and practice modern naval tactics. Their first naval battle was against China in the late 1800's when they defeated a larger fleet in the China Sea. In 1905, the Japanese Navy sank thirty five Russian warships in the battle of Tsushima Strait. This was the most decisive victory in a naval battle since the battle of Cape Trafalgar one hundred years earlier.

In 1908, American President Teddy Roosevelt became concerned with Japan's potential adventures in the Pacific and believed that they had intentions to start a war with the United States. In order to convince Japan of the folly of such a move, he ordered sixteen brand new American battleships and their escorts to make a round the world cruise, stopping at major ports along the way including Tokyo Bay, Japan.

It was obvious to everyone that he was trying to impress Japan with our inherent naval prowess and our superiority in naval strength. The cruise took fourteen months and was called, "The cruise of the "Great White Fleet." Japan seemed to be duly impressed, but the cruise mostly encouraged them to build a stronger navy of their own.

During World War I, Japan wisely joined with the Allies against

Germany and ended up at the end of the war with a gift of Pacific islands from the League of Nations. These islands included Palau, parts of The Marianas, Micronesia and The Marshall Islands. This transfer gave the Japanese important bases in the Pacific from which to launch their offensive against the U. S. twenty-two years later.

The Washington Naval Treaty of 1922 restricted the number of warships each country could build in hopes of preventing another war, but Japan renounced the treaty in the mid 1930's and went on a wild building spree. Japan obtained much of its warship steel from American junkyards. I can remember as a kid going down to the Oakland waterfront on the estuary and watching cargo ships flying the Japanese rising sun flag filling their holds with scrap steel from American foundries.

In 1936, the head of the San Francisco long shoreman's union, Harry Bridges, forbade his union members from loading Japanese ships with American scrap steel in the Bay Area. The conservative businessmen, bankers and industrialists in the area went wild and accused Bridges of being a Communist and working against American values. They tried to have him deported to his home country of Australia or jailed, neither of which worked. The Spanish Civil War in the mid 1930's raised the issue that to be against Hitler was to be pro Communist. Many people thought you were either one or the other.

Japan made its first move by invading Korea in 1910. Few paid much attention to it because Japan had previously invaded Korea twice in the sixteenth century and the two countries were only a few miles apart. And besides, they were both Asiancountries, so who in America should care. That was an attitude that was to prevail with us into World War II thirty years later. Japan moved into China invading Manchuria in 1931 and then expanded their control of China in 1937. We did nothing but watch, although the American public was slowly becoming more concerned about Japanese treatment of Chinese civilians

A Japanese Battleship

Anyone who looked could see that Japan was building for a war that would allow them to dominate Asia and the Pacific Ocean. However, Japan was an island nation, and war and domination of the area was not possible unless they could get control of sea routes and obtain supplies of needed food and raw materials.

To conduct a war they needed crude oil, tin, iron ore, coal, copper, aluminum (bauxite,) rubber and rice to name just a few. Fortunately for them all of these materials could be found in abundance in nearby Asian countries. All Japan had to do was conquer these weak countries and Asian dominance would be theirs. Japanese leaders considered this to be an easy task except for one thing, the U. S. Navy and its Pacific Fleet. The stage was being set for one of the greatest naval attacks of all time.

Still smarting from their ignominious defeat in World War I, Germany was preparing its people and armed forces for a new war, which they felt they could easily win. It was not easy to hide their intentions from neighbors and some countries were not fooled. However, no one outside Germany wanted another world war, so other European governments either shut their eyes to the obvious or decided that it was easier to join the Germans in their new adventure.

Most Americans saw what was happening in Europe, but many considered that it was Europe's problem in which we should not get involved. Roosevelt, and many Americans, felt that the world's only hope to defeat Hitler was in keeping England fighting hard and out of Hitler's hands. As mentioned in an earlier chapter, this was not the attitude of many Americans. Consequently, supporting England financially and militarily was a politically risky venture for President Roosevelt.

The worst situation would be to send billions of dollars of aid to England, and then have it all fall into Hitler's hands if England surrendered. Consequently, it was critical for Roosevelt to know if England would hold out or was likely to fold as other countries in Europe had done. To find out for himself, he selected his "best man", Joseph Kennedy, to be Roosevelt's new ambassador to England.

Forgive my negativity, but Joe was far from the best man for the job. He was probably the worst. In fact, his only qualification for becoming the ambassador to Great Britain was that he had raised the most money for Roosevelt's reelection campaign. Roosevelt needed an unbiased observer who could accurately measure the attitude and will of the English people to survive under all circumstances. What he got was an Irish Catholic who hated England to his core and was determined to keep American aid out of Britain. Some might disagree, but I believe the appointment of Joe Kennedy to the British Court was Roosevelt's worst mistake made during his presidency. Joe reported to the President that Hitler's takeover of England was only weeks away and that the English people would fold at the first sign of belligerence from Germany. Fortunately, and for reasons unknown to history, Roosevelt ignored Joe's advice and had him recalled. Roosevelt never spoke to Joe or gave him another job for the rest of his life.

It was extremely fortunate for the world that the President had the good sense or other information that caused him to ignore his special envoy to the British Court. This was one of those moments in history when the fate of civilization hung in the balance of someone making a correct decision. And he did. Kennedy's usefulness had run its course and his Irish Catholic roots almost sank the free world.

President Roosevelt took the dangerous course of helping the British to stay alive in spite of our country's overwhelming opinion against it. He never wavered in his belief that democracy's survival was at stake. But as the Forties approached, it was obvious to an increasing number of Americans that we would not be able to avoid a bloody confrontation that would probably cost us greatly. However, many conservatives were still not convinced. and fought to keep us unprepared in hopes that we could convince the Axis powers to spare us. It seems impossible today to conclude that any thinking American could have supported Hitler or ignored the coming threat from Japan, but many did. The Axis powers saw this internal American conflict and would read it to mean that we were vulnerable and unwilling to protect ourselves. They were going to discover their mistake very soon, but there would be many missteps and heavy casualties on both sides in the meantime.

Ambassador Joseph P. Kennedy

CHAPTER THREE

Crossing The Rubicon On The Way To War

A s we entered the 1940's, Axis countries correctly concluded that the Allies were confused and reluctant to join together in opposition to Germany, Italy and Japan. The three Axis countries had entered into a mutual protection pact and the United States seemed to be unwilling to join the Allies as an active partner. In Asia, the Japanese army had raped the women and children of Nanking, China, causing American public outrage, but their anger was not enough to go to war with Japan.

Hitler correctly surmised that his murder of millions of Jews would not stir anyone enough to respond. His belief was based on the lack of concern that the European powers showed for the Turkish murder of a million Armenian civilians in the First World War. So, everything was moving along for the Axis powers, and President Roosevelt was still unable to stir the American public to action.

However, the Japanese were shocked that the American public was beginning to stir in indignation against them due to the brutality of the Japanese army toward other Asians. There were even demands that the President do something to deter the Japanese army, everything, that is, short of war. As we moved into 1941, the President's war council noted that of all the raw materials needed by Japan, crude oil to operate their navy was in the shortest supply. Without going to war, shutting off Japan's oil supply seemed to be the act that would have the most immediate effect. At that time the U. S. and its allies had control of almost all of the crude oil in the world. Shutting off the oil supply to Japan would be no problem. So, the President gave Japan an ultimatum. "All of your crude oil is now shut off and will not be available to you again, unless you pull all of your troops out of China and the other Asian countries that you have invaded." The American public was happy that Japan would now have to give up its aggression and return home all without the U. S having to go to war. It was ingenious, except that the Japanese government didn't agree. They immediately sent their two best ambassadors to Washington to negotiate and also began to prepare for war with America. They had approximately nine month's supply of crude oil in storage in the fall of 1941.

Actually, they had been preparing for war since the Great White Fleet paid Japan a visit in 1908, but now preparations became serious. Something had to be done within the next nine months or they would be out of fuel. Everyone seemed to recognize this except the American public and our members of Congress.

In the Atlantic, the U. S. Navy was now escorting England bound convoys to a point approximately halfway across the Atlantic where they turned escort duties over to British destroyers and then turned toward home. In the fall of 1941, German submarines sank two of our escorting destroyers while they were on convoy duty, killing several dozen American sailors. Although this was without a declaration of war, it caused little stir in conservative America. The attitude of the anti-war group was that we should not be escorting ships to England in the first place, so it was all Roosevelt's fault.

At this point let's stop for a moment to remind the reader why America went to war against the Barbary Pirates of North Africa in 1801. President Jefferson had the support of the American public because the pirates were attacking and sinking American ships at will. We built a fleet of warships that wiped out the pirates in a couple of years. Compare this with the fact that German subs sank two of our warships killing dozens of American sailors in 1941, and the newspapers hardly mentioned it. Also, the U. S. entered World War I based on the sinking of the Lusitania by a German sub off Ireland in 1917. These are examples of how successful the conservative lobby was in lobbying the public against entering World War II or of helping any of our allies regardless of loss of American life. We had gone to two wars for less, but not in 1941.

The situation was getting serious on both oceans, but the conflict was not hot enough to cause us to help our friends. Let's now look closely at the political and global situation in the fall of 1941 in terms of what we knew, what we should have known and how all of this effected the events that followed.

CHAPTER FOUR

War Was Inevitable

A number of well-written books are available detailing the events that led up to the Pearl Harbor attack so I won't go into detail here. If you don't like to read, Tora, Tora, Tora, is an excellent movie accounting these events very accurately. It is important to outline here why neither President Roosevelt nor anyone else in the British or American governments knew about the impending attack. However, this still doesn't mean that we should have been caught napping.

The Japanese government was hoping that the United States would see the light and agree to Japan's move into Asia. But by 1941 the American public was in general agreement that Japan had to be stopped. The Japanese cruelty to its conquered neighbors prohibited the possibility of a negotiated settlement between Washington and Tokyo. That they thought that a negotiated settlement was a possibility seems ridiculous to us today, but the Japanese actually hoped to avoid war because of the slim possibility of a victory. The military government of Japan had convinced itself and its emperor that they must have all of Asia under their control at any cost. so, they made preparations for war.

Records available to us after the war show that the Japanese cabinet met often during the thirties to consider whether it was wise to continue their imperialistic policies or to retreat into their traditional role as a picturesque country with no international influence. They had felt for years that they were being treated as a second class power by the rest of the world, which, in fact, they were.

Since the military had taken over the cabinet, the outcome of their meetings would never be in doubt. Fortunately for some sanity, Fleet Admiral Yamamoto was a member of the cabinet. Unfortunately, his opinion was mostly ignored. He was known among American naval personnel who worked with him to be a skillful poker player and gambler. He also learned a great deal about American politics and culture while in Washington, and his views on going to war with us reflected this experience. He was apparently the only reasonable voice in the cabinet in those days. The Japanese army had control of the cabinet and thought that going to war with us would be no problem. They would learn to regret that viewpoint.

From what we know of those cabinet meetings, it appears that Yamamoto was unable to convince the generals that defeating America would not be possible for a small country like Japan. However, the cabinet agreed that a complete defeat of the U.S. was not necessary for the success of Japan's ultimate goal of controlling Asia. They believed that the only thing that stood between Japan and control of Asia was the U. S. Pacific Fleet. Some not so smart general concluded that all they had to do was sink our Fleet, and we would demand a negotiated settlement letting Japan have its way in Asia. This was the first of many stupid mistakes made by the Japanese before and during the war. However, the die was cast.

The generals turned to Admiral Yamamoto and asked him if the Imperial Navy could secure the Pacific long enough for Japan to conquer Formosa, The Philippines, French Indo China, The Dutch East Indies, Singapore, Hong Kong, Malaysia, Burma, Thailand, China and maybe even India. The Admiral is reported to have responded with the most realistic observation ever made about going to war. "I think we can control the seas for six months, maybe a year at most. After that, I can make no guarantees." His opinion was remarkably accurate since the U. S. Navy destroyed four of Japan's first line carriers just six months after Pearl Harbor in the famous battle of Midway.

Let's stop for a moment and summarize the situation that Japan found itself in during 1940-41. They had conquered Korea, Manchuria and many of China's major cities. They needed raw materials very badly, particularly crude oil and were staring at all of these materials in Southeast Asia just a few miles away. To pull their forces out of conquered lands would have been a serious embarrassment for the government and would have no doubt caused its political collapse. It is likely that the Japanese population, in a popular vote, would have demanded that they go to war with the U. S. rather than experience the humiliation of withdrawal from lands they had conquered. However, the Japanese people were never allowed to vote, so we will never know for sure how they felt. The cabinet could read its people and it was tired of being second class citizens in the world and it was willing to do something about the situation even though it realized that there was considerable risk involved.

The Japanese had spent years building up their navy and were very proud of their modern ships. In addition, they were convinced of the skills of their sailors and their devotion to their emperor. Bushido was their fighting code and every man in the army and navy knew what that meant to them. In fact, whenever anyone expressed concern about the size of America, the standard answer from anyone in Japan was, "Yes, but we have bushido."

None dared question that response or they would have been labeled a traitor.

Without going into too much detail, bushido meant to the Japanese that every Japanese fighting man was equivalent to at least five Americans. On top of this, Americans were depicted in the Japanese press as being weak, fun loving, unwilling to fight and were mostly fat. This raised the odds that one Japanese was equal to ten Americans. Admiral Yamamoto knew this was a fallacy, but no one was listening to him.

The Japanese also saw the naval balance that existed at the time. The American fleet was the second largest in the world behind only England's Royal Navy. However, our navy was divided between the two oceans that it had to protect. On top of that, our navy brass thought that our next enemy would be Nazi Germany so it kept most of its fleet in the Atlantic, especially its newer ships. But we had very few ships in either ocean that had been built since 1930 due to the conservatives in congress. They could see no point in spending good money on ships that would never be used; they were going to avoid war at all costs.

The Japanese Navy had a built in advantage; they had a larger more modern fleet with more aircraft carriers. Plus, they had been practicing for war since the twenties and had developed tactics and weapons that were far superior to ours. More about that later.

We started the war with seven aircraft carriers, two of which were built in the early 20's, and the Japanese had ten, all built in the 1930's and 40's. In addition, only three of ours were operating in the Pacific in 1941 with two, the Lexington and Yorktown, stationed at Pearl Harbor and the Saratoga in dry dock in Bremerton. The remaining four were operating in the Atlantic.

I won't go into detail about why we were so deficient in building aircraft carriers, the modern backbone of the fleet. Again, it was mostly a product of unwise financial frugality, but was also a result of old fashioned American Admirals who were living in the nineteenth century and still fighting with line of battle ships at the battle of Jutland. Fortunately, President Roosevelt could see into the future and had the navy design a new class of carrier, the Essex Class, that was destined to become the decisive weapon of the Pacific war. Twenty-four ships of the class were built during the war, but the first one, the USS Essex, was not operational until 1943.

By 1941, Japan could see that it had a significant advantage in naval strength in the Pacific, while we were concentrating on Germany and its submarine force. One could say that it was a tragic mistake not to have more ships stationed in the Pacific but the counter argument could be made that if we had, more ships would have been sunk by the Japanese at Pearl Harbor.

So, the Japanese had superior naval, army and air force weapons available at the start of the war. To the extent that this fact convinced them that a war with the U. S. was winnable we can't be sure. It is probable that it had a significant effect. If we had moved all our carriers and their support vessels into the Pacific in 1941 and sailed them up and down the Japanese coast, they may have thought twice before attacking Pearl Harbor. This was impossible for reasons that we will discuss next.

As mentioned earlier, the political situation in America was dynamite and the President was dancing a high wire act trying not to alienate anyone in the population or in the U.S. Congress. By 1940, the conservative drums, both southern and northern, were beating loudly. Roosevelt had met with Churchill, was sending war goods and food to both England and the Soviet Union, all in spite of severe criticism from the conservative press and Congress.

Their big complaint was that our President was trying to provoke both Japan and Germany into starting a conflict so that we could declare war. Many voters agreed, and our armed forces were warned to do nothing that might provoke our potential enemies into attacking us.

Confronting Japan with our formidable sea power was not an option. In fact, to be extra sure that we didn't "cross their bow" with anything that could be used as an excuse to start shooting, the President ordered our Pacific Fleet to stay in its base at Pearl Harbor. He could never be accused of starting World War II. Unfortunately, the demands of conservative lawmakers resulted in lack of training for our sailors and a predictable location for the bulk of our Pacific Fleet. Congress helped to keep our fleet in port by keeping its budget low for fuel oil in 1941.

The question has been sked, "Why did the President transfer the Pacific Fleet from its traditional home bases at Long Beach and San Diego, California out to Pearl Harbor, Hawaii in the late 1930's? He had a good reason so let's answer that question.

The average depth (draft) of the capital ships in the Pacific Fleet was 30 to 35 feet and the depth of the bay at Pearl Harbor is 40 to 45 feet. So, why is this important? This was a critical issue because of the characteristics of Japanese aerial torpedoes. When a torpedo was dropped from a Japanese bomber it would dive to depth of 60 to 70 feet before it would turn it up toward the surface. Our admirals knew this and were confident that the shallowness of the harbor would make the anchorage at Pearl Harbor the safest place for the Pacific Fleet to anchor in the world. Torpedoes would explode on the bottom of the bay and the ships would not be harmed.

Once again, our chauvinism toward Asian people caused unwarranted overoptimism as we refused to believe that the Japanese could find a solution to this problem. But, they did, and the solution was a brilliant piece of engineering. They built large fins on the tail of each torpedo that caused the torpedo, as soon as it hit the water, to turn upward and head for the surface. Consequently, the torpedoes dropped only fifteen to twenty feet down before returning to the surface . Not all of our ships were sunk by these torpedoes, but most were.

CHAPTER FIVE

Paying The Price For Frugality

I believe that the Japanese warlords wanted a war with the United States to prove to the world that they were a first class power and should be taken seriously. They had deluded themselves into thinking that they could destroy our Pacific Fleet in one swift blow and we would then sue for peace at their price. However, cooler heads had prevailed for the moment, and the cabinet agreed to send their two best envoys to Washington to negotiate one last time the terms that would avoid war.

As mentioned earlier, the Japanese military had been training for action for many months. Admiral Yamamoto had identified Pearl Harbor as the most logical location for a sudden strike that would sink our entire fleet that was almost always moored there. He was the architect of the attack and to be extra sure that all of our ships would be in port he selected Sunday, December 7, 1941 as the attack day. He almost correctly predicted that all the ships would be sure to be tied up, the sailors at rest and all weapons locked up or stowed away in their lockers.

Yamamoto sent his spies into Honolulu to keep him informed of the location and identity of all the ships in the harbor. His spies noted that the navy search planes always took off at 0800 every morning and not before. The few ships that were out on maneuvers during the week were always tied up at their assigned docks and anchorages during the weekend. Nothing changed, and the Japanese navy pilots were able to practice their low level attacks on known practice targets. Many pilots thought that sinking our ships was going to be easy. The Japanese fleet put to sea from a northern Japanese island and steamed eastward along a northern route toward Hawaii. They took this route because commercial sea traffic typically took a more southern route during winter to avoid storms. Our ship did that in the mid 1950's.

Radio silence was absolute and to insure this, they removed all of the short wave radios from the ships in the squadron. Only the flagship had its long distance radio intact and available. All ships had their TBS radios working but their operating range normally did not exceed twenty-five miles. More on this subject later.

Japanese Negotiators in Washington

Since we are discussing radio transmission, let's spend some time on the subject of code breaking and secret messages. As mentioned earlier, it was firmly established after the war that Japan never transmitted by radio their intent to attack Pearl Harbor. This fact was confirmed by searching through Japanese transmission records that are kept by all countries that use secret codes. There are logical reasons that confirm this conclusion:

- Who needed to know of the Japanese intent? Even Hitler was not told of the attack in advance.
- The final decision to launch the attack was not made until the fleet was halfway to Hawaii and the negotiations had collapsed in Washington
- Even the new Japanese Prime Minister was not told about the attack until the day before it happened.

Much has been written about the American's success in breaking the secret Japanese code before the war, so let's take a look at what really happened.

The U. S. Navy's code breakers in Honolulu, led by LCDR (later Captain) Joe Rochefort, did break the diplomatic code before the war, but not the naval code. They were different codes, and the IJN's code wasn't broken until the spring of 1942. As mentioned earlier, the diplomatic code record books show that no transmission was ever made of their intent to attack Pearl Harbor probably for the reasons listed above, plus one more:

Japanese Prime Minister Tojo

- No one in the Diplomatic Corps knew anything about the impending attack on Pearl Harbor. The two diplomats in Washington certainly didn't.

That leaves us with the Japanese naval code whose meaning was completely unknown to LCDR Rochefort and his crew before Pearl Harbor. However, there are two radio related incidents that need to be discussed. One is the story that ran through the U. S. Navy that our radio operators in Hawaii, even though they could not translate the code, were continually monitoring Japanese radio traffic between their ships anchored and steaming in Japanese waters. With experience, they could identify the name of the ship transmitting and its direction.

A couple of weeks before December 7th, the story goes that all of the radios in the Japanese battle fleet stopped transmitting at once and the Americans lost track of their location. Just before this loss, our radio operators reported that the Japanese battle fleet seemed to be preparing to get underway. They could tell this by the density of radio traffic, which always increases under these conditions.

When told of this, the officers at Honolulu are said to have reported to the admiral that the battle fleet was preparing to move south to invade Indonesia or some similar place. That conclusion confirmed the navy's belief that Southeast Asia would be Japan's first target when war started. However, due to the President's orders not to initiate engagement, nothing more was done. Everyone sat around and waited for the Japanese fleet to show up in the South China Sea.

LCDR Joe Rochefort

The second radio incident was reported to have occurred on the night of Saturday, December 6, 1941. The American Matson liner, SS Lurline, was just outside of Honolulu ready to tie up at the city docks the next morning. The radio operator was preparing to sign off and go to bed when he reportedly heard a strange transmission in a language, he didn't recognize at first. He turned up the volume and soon recognized that it was two or more Japanese ships talking to each other.

The Lurline's radio operator did not speak Japanese so he had no idea what was being said. He concluded that there was more than one ship involved in the conversation and decided to tell the authorities about it when they arrived in Honolulu the next morning. He then turned off his radio, left the radio shack and went to bed.

This incident is readily explained by anyone who has ever sailed in a navy ship in formation with other warships. As mentioned earlier, all long distance radios in the Japanese fleet were disabled except one on the flagship and no long distance transmission was possible. However, the TBS (talk between ships) radios were still active because their range was only twenty-five miles or so. There is an exception to their range however. Under certain atmospheric conditions the range of TBS radios can be inadvertently extended much further.

One night in 1954, my ship was steaming in formation with other attack transports several hundred miles off the San Diego coast. Suddenly we heard what appeared to be Spanish conversation coming over our TBS set. Our quartermaster on watch was of Mexican decent so I asked him to translate the conversation. He listened for a few minutes then broke into a smile. "Sir, that's two taxi cabs talking to one another in Tijuana." TBS radio waves can play tricks on you at night and travel several hundred miles and that is what happened to the Lurline on the night of December 6th, 1941. Unfortunately, a chance to prevent the coming attack was missed.

Depending on their speed, it takes ships between one and two weeks to travel between Japan and Hawaii. It was a stormy time of year so I imagine that the fleet did not travel fast through the rough seas. Japanese records inspected after the war confirms that when the fleet left northern Japan it had to maintain radio silence as mentioned earlier, but Tokyo could transmit all it wanted.

"The IJN staff at naval headquarters in Tokyo had made an agreement with the Fleet commanding officer, Admiral Nagumo. If Tokyo sent the message, "Climb Mount Nikitaka," it meant that the negotiations in Washington had failed and the fleet was to sail on and attack Pearl Harbor on December 7th as planned. The message was sent approximately a week before the fleet reached its destination and is the first time that the attack on Pearl was confirmed.

This was the first time that Japanese leaders knew for sure that they would attack the U. S. This is an important point to remember and provides another reason why they had not previously told anyone by radio that they were attacking Pearl Harbor. Although having trained for months for the possibility of an attack, they didn't know for sure it would take place until only a week before December 7th at the failure of the negotiations in Washington.

What was America doing during this time? A week before the attack the State Department had reached the conclusion that the negotiations with the two Japanese ambassadors were going nowhere. They had offered nothing new and were still demanding complete freedom to do what they wanted in Asia plus free access to all the oil they needed. The State Department notified the War Department and the War Department sent out a message to all Pacific bases to the effect that they should prepare for hostilities with Japan to break out at any moment. It's amazing that this official warning was ignored in Honolulu, but it mostly was.

So, let's summarize what the United States knew about the Japanese situation on December 1, 1941:

- Japan had only a few months of fuel left.
- Japan felt that the U.S. Pacific Fleet was their biggest obstacle to their imperialistic plans.
- The Japanese invasion fleet had left Japan and was headed south toward the Philippines.
- The Japanese battle fleet based in northern Japan had stopped radio transmission.
- The negotiations in Washington were going nowhere.

In summary, this is all that the president knew about the Japanese preparation for the war. The belief that the president knew in advance of the Japanese intention to attack Pearl Harbor is provably wrong on every level as previously discussed.

It is totally made up and continues to be claimed by people who should know better. Here are the facts which speak for themselves.

CHAPTER SIX

The Price Of Stupidity

I n the early 1930's, the U.S. Pacific Fleet was divided into two equal forces for their annual war games, the red fleet and the blue fleet. The red fleet was given Pearl Harbor to defend and the blue fleet made plans to attack it. It is said that the blue fleet made its attack on a Sunday morning before the search plane took off. The attacking planes dropped bags of flour on the unsuspecting ships of the red fleet tied up at dockside in the harbor. All were "sunk" and the blue fleet won the practice war games that year.

A second, more recent attack took place during the early months of World War II when a British fleet attacked the Italian fleet at Taranto, Italy sinking several of their large ships. One would have thought that our commanders in Pearl Harbor were aware of these strikes and would be prepared for them. But such was not the case.

To understand why, we need to look at the prejudice and racist attitude Americans had against the Japanese race in the 30's and 40's. When reminded of these successful surprise attacks, the common response was, "Yea, but they were carried out by American and British forces. The Japanese would never be capable of planning and executing such a complex attack." No, really. That was the prevailing view of the "inferior" Japanese then. To attack Pearl Harbor was far beyond the perceived capabilities of the "inferior race." We were a racist country.

USS Lexington Away From Pearl Harbor On Dec 7th

During this period, when my family's friends came over for Sunday dinner, the conversation always turned to the "upcoming conflict" with Japan. My dad, who had been in the cruiser navy in the early 1920's often said, "if they attack us, it will be a six weeks war, two weeks to find them, two weeks to sink them and two weeks to come home." This was a standard opinion of otherwise smart people before the war against the "second class race."

In any conflict, one can make two serious mistakes that can cost you victory. One is to underestimate your enemy. The other is to overestimate him. We did both at the lead up and in the early years of the war. And yes, our failure to accurately gauge the abilities and intentions of Japan almost cost us the war. It certainly cost us the loss of our battleships at Pearl Harbor. But the general and admiral in charge of Pearl Harbor defenses were only mirroring the attitude of the American public and members of Congress when they ignored the President's warning the week earlier. On December 6th, any American would have laughed at you if you had suggested that Japan was capable of carrying out such a complex attack. Because of our inherent racism, we were unable to protect ourselves from a well-planned sneak attack that crippled our Pacific Fleet.

There was another warning that, for technical reasons, did not get to Honolulu in time, and this too was caused by a failure in radio transmission.

As mentioned earlier, we had broken the Japanese diplomatic code and were eavesdropping on the messages being sent between Tokyo and its negotiators in Washington. On the morning of December 7th, before the attack took place, Tokyo radioed its people in Washington to destroy all records before 1:00PM Washington time (8:00AM Honolulu time) and then ask for a meeting with the American Secretary of State, Cordell Hull.

The American code breakers thought that something serious was going to happen at 1:00 PM so immediately alerted the administration about the message. The Japanese envoys had no idea what was up but they immediately went to work. Then a message came through from Tokyo that the negotiators were to draft a declaration of war against the U.S. and present it to the secretary at their 1:00PM meeting.

Unfortunately, the Japanese secretary on duty in their office was a poor typist and took longer to type the important letter. But now the Americans knew of the impending war declaration, and the President ordered that an emergency message be sent to all Pacific bases of the impending declaration of war. So, a radio transmission was immediately sent to Pearl Harbor, but the transmission was unsuccessful! It was one of those rare days when the ionosphere was falling apart and long distance radio waves were not being reflected back to earth. So, the

War Department finally succeeded by sending the message to Western Union for transmission. However, someone had forgotten to mark "urgent" on it. So, it was transmitted as a routine message. Here was another costly mistake made by no one of importance.

The Japanese attack on Pearl Harbor has always been characterized as a "sneak" attack because, when it happened, war had not been declared. This was obviously not Japan's intention. They had planned that Secretary Hull would be presented with the war declaration at the moment the Japanese planes fell out of the sky onto our unsuspecting fleet. This had to be timed just right so that the Americans didn't have time to prepare but that we could not accuse the Japanese of attacking without warning. It didn't work this way, but planning that the timing would be just right for such an event was gross wishful thinking. In any case, the warning from Washington arrived by Western Union messenger an hour after the attack had started.

Two other missed events happened that fateful morning that could have prevented or mitigated the attack, one by the navy and one by the army. A new radar unit had just been installed on a nearby mountaintop and was in operation that morning. The operator was new, and radar was basically unknown in our military in 1941, but it was operating perfectly when the operator announced to his partner that he had picked up a large flight of planes headed toward Hawaii from the north.

His partner called the army officer on watch at the base and told him of the radar contact. The officer replied that there was a flight of B-17's coming in from California that morning and that was probably what they had picked up, so the operator shut down the radar unit and headed back to the base. This conclusion was obviously wrong because California is northeast of Hawaii not due north. The officer in charge was off by forty- five degrees.

The second event occurred at sea just outside the entrance to the harbor. At 0630 hours on the morning of the 7th the American destroyer, the USS Ward, a leftover from WW I, spotted and attacked an unidentified midget submarine trying to follow another navy ship into the harbor. The destroyer's captain reported to the base that they had fired several shots from their five inch guns and dropped depth charges on a submarine. The fact that there was an unknown sub in the area was confirmed by another ship and a PBY scout airplane flying overhead at the time. The report was passed up to Admiral Kimmel, but he chose to ignore it barely one hour before the attack.

It's hard to say what would have happened differently if either or both of these reports had been acted on, but it's likely that American interceptors would have been in the air and ships' anti-aircraft guns manned and ready. I think that the outcome would have been different.

Japanese Aircraft Carrier

CHAPTER SEVEN

The Captain Always Goes Down With His Ship

T he military has an honored tradition that the commanding officer of a ship or combat unit has the ultimate responsibility for the safety of that unit and the men in it. No excuses are acceptable. The administration alerted the Pacific military bases to the possibility of hostilities a full week before the attack on Pearl Harbor, but Admiral Kimmel and General Short did nothing to prepare. They ignored the warning. Their racism and sheer stupidity kept them from preparing for the attack that the State Department earned might be coming, except by sending the Lexington and Yorktown to Wake Island to deliver fighter planes.

However, it doesn't matter whether they were alerted or not; it is the time-honored tradition in the military that the commanding officer must always do whatever is appropriate to protect his base or ship. Not doing so is a court martial offense, but the two were demoted and relieved of command instead, and retired the next year. Conservative members of Congress have tried over the years to relieve them of responsibility for the attack on Pearl Harbor. These are the same men who hated President Roosevelt and tried to keep us unprepared for war in the 1930's and 40's.

When my dad heard of the attack, he commented to me that when his ship was stationed at Pearl Harbor in 1925, there were fighter planes flying overhead continuously to protect the fleet from air attack, even though we were not at war with anyone.

The Admiral and General stood for a congressional inquiry and were rightly found derelict in their duty for failure to take appropriate action to protect their men, ships and base. Since then, conservatives who don't like President Roosevelt have been claiming that the two were railroaded and the President should have been blamed. Hogwash! They were warned a week in advance, but that was irrelevant. There is never an acceptable excuse for being unprepared for an attack in either peace or war. Any military man should know that. If you are not willing to accept that fact, then you should not accept the responsibility of command.

This concept was demonstrated in the aftermath of the sinking of the USS Indianapolis in the summer of 1945. The details of the tragic sinking of the heavy cruiser that brought the two atomic bombs to Saipan are too well known to discuss here. The story of the Indianapolis is relevant to Pearl Harbor because of the fact that the ship's captain was court marshaled for not taking evasive action while steaming to the Philippines even though the war was just two days from ending

The captain testified that he had requested destroyer escort but it had been denied. The Japanese sub captain testified that the cruiser could have taken no evasive action that would have prevented him from scoring a direct hit with his torpedoes.

Nevertheless, the captain was convicted because he lost his ship although many people who are familiar with the case were very critical of the navy's verdict.

So, let's put to bed the controversy of who was responsible for the Japanese "sneak" attack on Pearl Harbor. Its success was the result of a combination of good planning by Admiral Yamamoto, good (but not great) execution by Admiral Nagumo, bad luck and bad judgment on the American side and incompetence by the two commanding officers of the base, which was caused mostly by racist denial of the abilities of the Japanese.

One last item concerning the attack needs to be discussed. Although most of America's luck was bad on that fateful Sunday morning, two events that happened that day saved the war for the United States on the day that it started.

Because the War Department had alerted Pearl Harbor that war was probably imminent, Admiral Kimmel ordered his two aircraft carriers and their escorts to deliver fighter planes to Wake Island. Consequently, the USS Yorktown and USS Lexington and their escort ships were not in Pearl Harbor on the 7th. Also the light cruiser USS Richmond had been sent to South America on a goodwill mission. Had they been at Pearl they would certainly have been sunk crippling our fleet even more than it was. (The cruiser .USS Raleigh, sister ship of the Richmond, was tied up at her dock during the attack and took three torpedoes during the attack. Due to a heroic effort by her crew she stayed afloat and survived the war. A young man who lived on our block in Oakland was in the crew of the Raleigh and told me that story.)

As a result of this good fortune, all of our fleet carriers were available after December 7th to begin counter attacks. Both carriers were involved in the Coral Sea battle that turned the Japanese away from Australia. The Lexington was sunk in that battle but the damaged Yorktown was repaired and participated in the battle of Midway where it was also sunk. By the Battle of Midway the carriers Hornet and Enterprise had joined the Pacific Fleet from the Atlantic so that three carriers were available for the Midway battle.

The second bit of good fortune was a decision by Japanese Admiral Nagumo. Yamamoto's original plan called for the attacking planes to return to their carriers, refuel, rearm and make a second strike at Pearl. This second strike was to destroy the dry docks and the many fuel storage tanks scattered on the nearby hills.

For reasons Admiral Nagumo never discussed except with his boss, Admiral Yamamoto, he decided that the Americans were alerted by the first attack and would be waiting for them if they returned for a second strike. He ordered his ships to turn around and head home without attacking again. His failure to destroy the dry docks and the fuel depot was a monumental blunder that angered Admiral Yamamoto and the sailors in his fleet. Admiral Nagumo was an old man, probably the oldest man in the Japanese navy and lacked the fire and bravado to take a chance that would have kept us out of the Pacific for months or maybe years to come.

It was said after the war that if the Japanese had destroyed our navy's fuel supplies at Pearl, we would have been unable to put a fleet to sea for at least nine months, maybe twelve. Also, because our dry docks were left intact, all of our sunken ships except one were repaired and back in action within two years.

It is interesting to note that three important battles happened within the first nine months of the Pearl Harbor attack: Coral Sea, Midway and the invasion of Guadalcanal. None of these would have been possible if the Japanese had destroyed our fuel supply.

At the battle of Surigao Straight in October of 1944, Admiral Jesse Oldendorf lead six battleships and sank all but one of the Japanese ships including two battleships. All but one of Oldendorf's battleships had been sunk and raised at Pearl Harbor and repaired by the dry docks that Admiral Nagumo should have destroyed.

Mistakes cost countries wars and America's mistakes were bad enough to permit Japan to mount a successful attack on Pearl Harbor. But Japan's mistakes at the beginning and during the war cost them victory while suffering huge casualties.

Their first and biggest mistake was to attack Pearl Harbor in the first place. I think Admiral Yamamoto knew this and tried to inject a modicum of sanity in Japan's discussions in the 30's and 40's on declaring war as mentioned earlier. The conclusion that the Japanese cabinet made that the U. S. would be forced into peace negotiations after our fleet was sunk at Pearl was the costliest mistake made by anyone in history.

As the United States was racist, so was Japan. They looked upon Americans as inferior, sloppy and lazy cowards. Yamamoto's comment after the attack was very accurate when he was reported to have said that they had "Awakened a sleeping giant." He knew that they had bit off more than Japan could chew, but he was patriotic enough to do what his government decided. Japan underestimated America's ability, resolve and determination to avenge the attack on our sleeping navy, the first of many costly mistakes made by Japan.

CHAPTER EIGHT

If You're Going to Attack, Do It Right

Once Japan had decided to attack the United States, they should have done it right. Just to "awaken a sleeping giant," as Admiral Yamamoto put it, was not only ineffective, it was dangerous. America could have been knocked out of the war by attacking us on the West Coast, but not by sinking a few old battleships at Pearl Harbor and tweaking the giant's beard.

We have to accept the fact that we were dangerously unprepared. This was no more apparent than along our West Coast including Washington, Oregon but mostly in California. Northern California had been a location for many important military bases, some dating as far back as the Civil War. From the Bremerton navy Yard in Washington to the Destroyer Base in San Diego, there would have been nothing left from which to mount a counter attack against Japan. If Admiral Nagumo had continued on from Hawaii to San Francisco, less than a week's sail, he could have caused havoc from which we might never have recovered. There was no protection for our west coast military bases once the capital ships at Pearl had been sunk. Neither did we have any planes for air protection from either the Army or Navy.

It was said that the reason that Nagumo fled Hawaii as quickly as he did was because of the two American Aircraft carriers that were somewhere between Honolulu and Wake Island. But let's be real. Our carriers and their marginally trained airmen, as much as we loved them, were no match for Japan's experienced combat pilots. Most had fought in China and were experienced in flying and fighting as we saw at Pearl Harbor. Nagumo was not willing to take significant losses so he ordered a complete retreat while our West Coast lay at his feet waiting to be obliterated. His actions guaranteed Japan's defeat. It was just a matter of time. It was not clear that even Admiral Yamamoto saw the chance that his fleet had missed. Many of us who lived in California saw clearly what they could have done and we were terrified.

It was obvious to those of us living in California that Japanese forces would continue on eastward and finish the job, and there was nothing we could do to stop them. There were blackouts in the Bay Area, and we kids hid under our desks to keep from being killed by Japanese bombs. In addition, we always looked up when a plane flew overhead. If the Japanese had continued on to our Bay Area, they could have destroyed the majority of America's war making capability, including:

- Hunter's Point Naval Shipyard that possessed the largest crane in the world able to lift entire engines out of battleships for repair.
- Fort Mason, through which many of the troops headed for the Pacific embarked.
- The docks along the San Francisco waterfront, across which much of the military cargo passed during the war.
- Moffett Field Naval Air Station in Sunnyvale, the home of the dirigible squadrons that patrolled the Pacific Coast attacking and sinking Japanese submarines.
- Alameda Naval Air Station, from which Colonel Doolittle initiated his famous but minimally effective raid on Tokyo.
- Oakland Naval Supply Center, the largest supply center in the world.
- Oakland Army Terminal, through which passed all

the Army personnel heading into the Pacific theatre.

- Two major shipyards on the Alameda estuary, Todd Shipyard and Moore Drydock.
- The Mare Island Naval Shipyard that had been building and repairing ships and submarines since the Civil War.
- Concord Naval Weapons Depot, through which passed all of the ammunition used by the Navy and Marine Corps in the Pacific Island campaigns.
- Kaiser Shipyards in Richmond that built most of the Liberty, tanker and Victory ships for the war.
- Naval Fuel Depot in Richmond that supplied all the gasoline, diesel and bunker fuel used in the Pacific.
- Treasure Island, headquarters of the Twelfth Naval District.
- Yerba Buena Island Coast Guard base.
- Three major West Coast oil refineries in Contra Costa County.
- Ford and Chevrolet assembly plants that manufactured jeeps and trucks in Oakland and Richmond.
- And not to be forgotten, the two bridges that span the bay into San Francisco. The destruction of these bridges would have bottled up the bay for years.

The Japanese did not attack our West Coast, and their fate was sealed.

Interestingly, all of the conservative criticism of the President for trying to take us into war by preparing for it suddenly stopped on December 7th. The Charles Lindbergs and Father Coughlins of our country stopped whining and climbed on board the war effort. Father Coughlin was nowhere to be found; the damage they had done to President Roosevelt's attempts to prepare for war was immense but incalculable. The Japanese bombs and torpedoes pulled us together like nothing else could. We were finally in this together. The failure to attack our west coast was probably Japan's biggest mistake of all.

It is interesting to note that when the war started, as mentioned in an earlier chapter, President Roosevelt ordered his air corps not to permit Charles Lindberg to enlist. So, he went to work for Lockheed in Southern California ferrying P-38's to the South Pacific. He has the record for being the only civilian to shoot down enemy planes. He had two Zeroes to his credit.

The Fuel Storage Tanks Survived the Attack on Pearl Harbor

CHAPTER NINE

Bring Your Friends
To The Party

As mentioned earlier, Adolph Hitler knew nothing in advance that Japan planned to attack Pearl Harbor. One can only imagine his confusion and surprise when he heard about it. We must remember that after December 7th we were still not at war with Germany, confusing the pro-Nazi Americans. Their typical response was, "Let England and Russia fight Germany and we will fight Japan." There was a lot of hopeful thinking in that viewpoint by America's pro German sympathizers because there seemed to be no reason for Hitler to attack us.

For the next several days Hitler worried about what he was going to do about the U. S. There has been a lot written about exactly why he eventually declared war on the United States. Four days after Pearl Harbor, on December 11th, he announced in a broadcast that Germany was declaring war on the United States. That solved a lot of problems for the U.S. because the pro-German group in our midst finally had to admit that Hitler was our enemy; the United States was finally at war with Germany.

The question no one has been able to answer is why did Hitler declare war on us when there was really no need to. He was deep into Russia and on the doorstep of Moscow that winter. Some people have speculated that he needed Japanese raw materials, or that he wanted

Japan to invade Siberia from the east. We don't know, but my belief is that he had several reasons.

First of all, he saw the destruction of the American fleet at Pearl Harbor and thought that beating the U.S. would be a pushover. He also saw the division in the American public that we have talked about earlier and thought that a majority of Americans would not be willing to fight Germany. Also, Hitler had a mutual defense pact with Japan that bound him to support Japan if anyone attacked it, but we hadn't done the attacking, so that didn't apply.

Hitler had made a fatal mistake in attacking the Soviet Union the previous summer and made his second serious mistake by declaring war on the U. S. that winter. Why he did it is anybody's guess, but now he was at war with the Soviet Union, the British Isles, Canada, Australia, New Zealand, India, South Africa and the United States. Even though, in the winter of 1941-42 , the war was looking good for the Axis.

In 1942 the German war against the U.S consisted of submarine action; the sinking of our ships was serious to both the British and Soviets as well as to our merchant marine. We now had a war on both coasts. The year 1942 was not a good one for us. We did win some battles and began to take the war to our enemies. Now let's discuss the weapons and tactics on both sides as the war opened.

German Submarine on Patrol in The Atlantic

CHAPTER TEN

How We All Compared

To understand fully our dilemma in fighting the Axis powers in 1941, we need to review the condition of our weapons and how each compared with those of the Axis powers. Remember, our congress had consistently refused to allocate sufficient funds to modernize and equip our fighting forces. Let's take a look at where that put us when the war began. In other words, who had the best weapons on Dec. 7th, 1941.

Fighter Planes

Japan. The Zero was probably the best fighter plane in the world in 1941. It was fast, maneuverable and had a good rate of climb. No Allied fighter at the time could stand up to it except probably the Spitfire. The Zero was well designed and easy to build, but lacked armor to protect the pilot and they came apart easily when hit by .50 caliber machine gun fire. It was outclassed by both the Navy's Hellcat and the Army's Mustang beginning in 1943. But in 1941-42 the Zero ruled the skies in the Pacific.

The United States. The Army had the P-40 and the Navy the F4F Wildcat. Both were adequate but neither was a match for the Zero or the German Me-109. The P-38 was superior to the Zero in many respects but did not become operational until well into 1942. The Navy's Corsair was a good fighter, but was not usable aboard aircraft carriers until well into the war. It was a good Marine fighter though, and was later developed by the British for carrier use.

The Japanese Zero Fighter Plane

The Army's P-40 Warhawk

U.S. Navy's F4F Wildcat Fighter Plane

Germany. TThe ME-109 was developed during the 30's and was an excellent fighter. No American plane could match it until the P-47's and P-51's became operational in 1943. However, the Spitfire proved its match during the Battle of Britain in 1940.

The Messerschmitt Me-109

The Folke Wolf 190 was an air cooled radial engine fighter that was superior to the Spitfire in every way except for turning. Its twin 20mm cannons and two heavy machine guns gave it much more fire power than the puny .303 caliber machine guns on the Spitfire. As the war went on the Brits caught on and added two 20mm cannons to their Spitfire, but we are comparing fighter planes in 1941. RAF pilots learned early on to avoid the 190 whenever possible.

Great Britain. The RAF's Spitfire was the best designed fighter in the European war until the P-51 arrived in 1943. It usually out-performed the ME-109 in combat. Its design was based on racing seaplanes that Supermarine Company had built during the 30's that had dominated the speed races before the war. The Spitfire had pretty much the same body without the pontoons. The Rolls Royce Merlin engine was the best internal combustion engine ever built and made the Spitfire the best fighter plane in Europe. Unfortunately, it had a limited range and was unable to escort its bombers to Germany and back. It really took off (no pun intended) when 100 octane gasoline (and later 130 and 150 octane gasoline) became available along with the increase in the Merlin's compression ratio (see chapter 16).

The RAF's Spitfire Fighter

Soviet Union The MIG fighter was adequate but usually outclassed by the German ME-109. It improved as the war went on.

The Russian MIG Fighter Plane
Fighter Plane Advantage: Japan/Germany

Long Range Bombers

Japan/Germany. Neither Japan nor Germany developed long range four engine bombers before or at the beginning of the war. Their medium bombers were used for long range bombing missions but their bomb loads were small.

United States. The U.S. Air Corps started the war with a partially developed Boeing B-17. It was the world's early four engine bomber and, although it proved to be very effective, was over designed and consequently could not carry a large bomb load. The follow-on B-24 and later B-29 were superior in design and bomb carrying capacity.

U.S. Army's B-17 Bomber Note the wing's low aspect ratio

Great Britain.

The RAF had one of the best long-range bombers at the start of the war in the Avro Lancaster. It had a high aspect ratio wing, carried a large bomb load and was powered by four Merlin engines.

Advantage: U.S./Great Britain

Medium Range Bombers

Both the Axis and the Allies had good medium range bombers when the war started. The RAF developed the best medium range bomber in the Mosquito, but it wasn't available until later in the war. When operational, it was the fastest propeller driven plane ever built.

United States

The B-25 Mitchell was our workhorse medium bomber all during the war and was used until the Korean Conflict. It was the bomber used by General Doolittle in his raid on Tokyo in 1942.

Germany

The standard German bomber used during the war was the Henkel He-88. It was originally designed to support troops but was ultimately used to bomb England for which it was not originally intended.

Advantage: Neither side until the Mosquito came out, then the Allies.

The RAF's Mosquito Medium Range Bomber The two Merlin engines made it the fastest Propeller driven plane ever built

US Army's B-25 Billy Mitchell Medium Bomber Work horse of the USAAF

Germany's He-88 Medium Bomber

Tanks

Germany. Although the tank was invented in World War I by the British, the Germans were the leaders in tank design during WW II beginning with the Panzer I, II and III, and transitioning to the Panther and Tiger designs later on. German tanks had maintenance problems and were difficult to repair and were out of service for long periods when damaged.

United states The M4 Sherman was a good medium tank but was no match for the heavy German tanks. It was said that it took at least six Shermans to destroy one Panther and five of them did not survive. Only the one coming up from behind the Panzer tank lived to fight again.

Tiger 1 German Tank

General Patton was criticized for approving the Sherman medium tank when many of the German tanks, the Tiger and the Panther, were larger and heavier gunned. But Patton's critics failed to understand that the Sherman tank was the heaviest tank that could be lifted abord a cargo ship and transported across the Atlantic. Yes, it is true that the big German tanks would prevail in one on one combat, but most of the German armies used smaller tanks that the Sherman could defeat. The Sherman also did a great job in infantry support, and many experts believe that the Sherman was the best tank as the war wore on, but in 1941 the Germans had the best tank.

Great Britain. The Churchill tanks were well designed and when outfitted with the 75 mm gun were effective in most tank battles. It did not have sufficient armor to stand up to the Panther, however.

Japan. Japan had no experience in building tanks and bought several hundred from France before the war. The tanks they finally built were inferior and lightly armored and were no match for the American's Sherman. A friend of mine who was a machine gunner in the infantry said that his biggest problem in fighting a Japanese tank was that they were so lightly armored that his .30 caliber bullets would penetrate through the tank's armor, go through the tank and injure or kill American troops on its other side.

Soviet Union. The Russians developed their T-34 tank in great secrecy and sprung it on the Germans in the battle of Kursk, the largest tank battle in history. They were not quite equivalent to the German Panther but did destroy many of them. They won the battle of Kursk and lead the Soviet army into Germany.

Advantage: Germany

U.S. Army's Sherman Medium Tank

Russia's T-34 Tank

Germany's 88mm Field Artillery Gun

Field Artillery

Germany. The Germans had developed what was considered to be the best artillery weapon in the war, the 88mm. It was the only artillery piece that could be used for infantry support, anti-tank action and anti-aircraft fire.

United States. The U.S. Army used mostly 75mm, 105mm and 155mm field artillery and separate 90mm anti-aircraft guns. None of these matched Germany's 88.

Advantage: Germany

Navy

Great Britain. The Royal Navy was the largest in the world, but most of its large ships were of WW I vintage. They had to split it into the Mediterranean Fleet, the Home Fleet, the Atlantic Fleet and the Pacific Fleet. The Pacific Fleet was decimated when the Japanese sank the Prince of Wales and the Repulse in the first week of the war. The home fleet was kept near Britain to prevent Germany from invading. Their most serious defects were made obvious by the Bismarck's sinking of the HMS Hood in 1941 with a single shell that ignited the Hood's ammunition storage.

Germany. The German navy was small but very modern since most of its ships were built during the 30's and 40's. The ships were well designed and the crews were skillful. Fortunately for the Allies, Hitler was afraid to commit them very often so they had marginal effect on the war. Germany's most important ship was the submarine that raised havoc with Allied shipping until 1943 when the Allied anti-submarine warfare force in the Atlantic finally overwhelmed them. Their submarines were well designed for long range patrols and their tactics were designed to bring England to its knees, which they almost did.

Hitler was so afraid to commit his surface navy that he kept his largest battleship, the Deutschland, anchored in a fjord in Norway until it was finally sunk near the end of the war by British Mosquito bombers.

Royal Navy's HMS Barham

Japan. Japan had ignored the restrictions on her naval size imposed by the Washington Conference in 1922 and built it up frantically during the 1930's. They had six heavy aircraft Carriers and six light carriers plus seven carriers under construction. In addition, Japan had ten battleships with three under construction. Two of their battleships, the Yamato and the Musashi, were the largest warships ever built. Japan had only the Pacific Ocean to patrol.

Note: When the Yamato was sunk by U.S. Navy dive bombers and torpedo bombers in 1945, over 3000 Japanese sailors went down with her, almost the same number as the total number of Americans killed in the Japanese attack on Pearl Harbor.

The Japanese advantage went far beyond its ships. It had developed torpedoes during the 30's that were deadly and far superior to America's. The Type 93, or Long Lance, as they were called, had a longer range, higher explosive charge and were faster, more accurate and pretty much undetectable on the way to their target. They were undetectable and faster because they used pure oxygen as the oxidizer to power the propulsion turbine. Using pure oxygen was something the U.S. Navy never developed for its torpedoes. Pure oxygen left no wake making the approaching torpedo almost invisible. Most of the battleship sunk at Pearl Harbor were sunk by the Long Lance plus the following Allied carriers and cruisers: Northampton, Juneau, Hornet, Yorktown, Atlanta, Wasp, Helena, Houston, Exeter, Perth, Java, De Ruyter plus ten destroyers.

Germany's Battleship Bismarck

The second advantage that the Imperial Japanese Navy had was in their training for war at sea. Their tactic was to turn their destroyers "loose" during sea battles and let them roam free in between American ships to discharge their torpedoes. American tactics kept their destroyers in line with the capital ships rendering them pretty much useless in combat. This was changed when Admiral Arleigh Burke took command of our destroyer squadrons in 1943.

The third advantage for the IJN was in their binoculars. They had developed binoculars that could "see" at night and proved to be very effective before radar was developed.

These three technical advances gave the IJN a distinct advantage over the United States Navy in the Pacific in 1941.

Japanese Battleship Yamato. Largest warship in the world

United States. The United States had two oceans to guard and the ships stationed in the Pacific to fight the Japanese were as follows: nine battleships, three aircraft carriers, eleven heavy cruisers, and ten light cruisers according to Wikipedia. Of our three carriers in the Pacific, two, the Lexington and Saratoga, were launched in the early 1920's and were built from heavy cruiser hulls. Our Pacific Fleet was outdated in 1941 and it was significantly outclassed by a superior, modern fleet manned by well trained Japanese crews.

Battleship U.S.S. California Rebuilt after being sunk at Pearl Harbor

Japan's attack on Pearl Harbor was to have sunk the Lexington and

Yorktown that had been stationed there. In a stroke of unusually good luck, as mentioned earlier, they were both at sea delivering planes to Wake Island on December 7th and were spared the fate of their sister ships sitting at anchor in the harbor. The Saratoga was in dry dock in Bremerton being refitted.

It took several months for the U.S. to transfer its modern capital ships from the Atlantic to the Pacific. Our first victory in the Pacific happened in May of 1942 in the Coral Sea and our big victory happened in June at Midway. We were otherwise pushed around badly and lost several sea battles at Guadalcanal until a year after Pearl Harbor.

Speaking of the Pacific war, the question can be asked how did we win it at all when one looks at how badly outclassed we were in December of 1941. The answer, as all historians will tell us, is in our ability to get unified, organized and productive, plus we had a little luck. By a year after Pearl Harbor we were launching the new Essex class aircraft Carriers, the North Carolina and the South Dakota class battleships soon followed by the four Iowa class battleships, our largest warships.

This was all happening because our basic divide over the war was eradicated by the Japanese "sneak" attack in December. For one of the few times in our history we were all pulling in the same direction. Even those anti-war conservatives who had made life so difficult for Roosevelt in the 1930's joined in to defeat the Axis. The "sleeping giant" in all its glory was truly awakened.

Advantage: Japan until the Essex class carriers were built.

CHAPTER ELEVEN

A Plan That Could Have Worked

The main point of this book is that, with a little planning, a proper knowledge of the American psyche and listening to the people who knew, the Japanese high command could have executed a war plan that might easily have succeeded. It seems obvious to us now, but it eluded the Japanese high command completely in 1941.

So, let's assume that we were the Japanese High Command in 1941 and were planning a war with the U.S. The first thing we should do is outline our goal clearly and distinctly.

Goal

The primary goal of Japan in the 40's was to dominate Asia and control its resources and people. It is an island nation and has almost no resources of its own. Americans completely misunderstood this and thought that the Japanese wanted to conquer the U.S. and "dictate surrender terms on the steps of the White House," as Admiral Yamamoto was misquoted as saying. (He actually said that Japan could never defeat the U.S. unless they could dictate, etc. His actual comments had an entirely different meaning and once again he was right.)

Obstacle

The most formidable obstacle to accomplishing this goal was perceived by the General Staff to be the U.S. Pacific Fleet. However, as noted earlier, the U.S. Pacific Fleet would have been no match for the modern Japanese Navy in a head to head battle in December of 1941. In actuality, the most formidable obstacle to Japan's plans was American strength and resolve. Before Japan attacked Pearl Harbor, we had neither and Japan's military leaders failed to see the importance of that deficiency.

As mentioned earlier, half of the population of the U.S. would not have wanted to go to war with Japan in December of 1941. Japan didn't know it but they could have done pretty much whatever they wanted in the Pacific short of attacking us without reprisal.

Unfortunately for Japan, they did the one thing that brought Americans together to wipe them out, attack America without warning. So, what could Japan have done in 1941 to accomplish its goal of dominating Asia? Let's plan a campaign as if we were Japanese who really understood America and Americans.

A Plan That Would Have Worked

Let us (Japan) now assemble a mighty fleet and sail south toward (what is today) Indonesia and Malaysia, bypassing the Philippines and ignoring the U.S. Pacific Fleet moored at Pearl Harbor. In the center of our fleet we will put troop transports and other support auxiliaries. Surrounding the transports will be our magnificent aircraft carriers with planes on board ready to take off at a moment's notice. Our battleships and cruisers will surround the carriers. The outer ring will be made up of destroyers to protect against American submarine attack.

Our submarine force will be distributed every few hundred miles in a line between our fleet and Pearl Harbor to warn of any movement toward us by the ships of the U.S. Fleet.

Australia

As we head south, we could continue on and invade Australia. Although Australia is an independent country, it is a part of England and it is not actually a part of our plan for Asia domination. Japan will have access to all of the resources it needs without invading Australia. However, defeating a Caucasian country here in Asia will have great political and propaganda effect. Let's play this one by ear and see if it would be to our ultimate advantage to invade Australia without provoking the U.S.

India

The conquest of India is not a part of this initial plan. However, if things work out, our armed forces will end up on the Burma border facing the eastern edge of India. There is great dissatisfaction among Indian people with their English rulers and many would gladly join our invasion forces to throw the English out. We should be ready to move on westward if circumstances point toward an immediate victory in India.

The Philippines

The Philippines could be a problem if the U.S. decides to use it as a base to attack our fleet with high altitude bombers. This is a minor threat because no ship was ever sunk during the war by high altitude bombers in spite of what American propaganda says. The Philippines have no resource value to Japan and would only require that Japanese troops be stationed there and unavailable for use where they are really needed. Its conquest might have a propaganda value, however.

Propaganda

As our fleet sails south, we tell the American people that what we are doing does not involve them. We are only taking valuable resources away from imperialistic European countries like England, Holland and France for the good of the indigenous people of Asia. We remind them that our striking force is the largest that has ever been assembled and other countries (like the U.S.) should stay clear of it. Any attempt to stop us would be doing so for the benefit of the three imperialistic European countries that the U.S. has refused to help in Europe. Why should the U.S. care what happens to them?

As we sail past the Philippines, we put our carrier fighter planes in the air in case the Americans foolishly decide to intervene. Our submarines would quickly alert us if their ancient fleet at Pearl Harbor attempted to intercept us. We would immediately move our warships to a formation along the northeast edge of our formation and be ready to sink any ships that tried to interfere with our southerly progress. However, the Pearl Harbor ships could not get organized and move quickly enough to interfere even if they wanted to, which they probably wouldn't.

The three European countries whose Asian countries would be taken are in no condition to fight back. Holland and France have been overrun and surrendered to Hitler, and England is fighting for its life against Germany.

So the world would be faced with a fete accompli and Japan would have the resources it needs to dominate Asia as planned. The United States would be faced with a decision to attack us with a weaker fleet or let things go as they are. But if our plans work out, the American public will not be tempted to intervene because our invasion of Southeast Asia would not directly affect them. We have accomplished our objective!

CHAPTER TWELVE

America's Response To Our Make-Believe Attack

T he important prospect of success of this plan would be in America's response to the invasion of Southeast Asia by a huge Japanese fleet. Remember, as a major part of this plan, the Japanese would not attack Pearl Harbor. Let's dig deep into the American psyche during the period and see what might have been its response.

As mentioned earlier, almost half of the American population was against war at all costs. If our plan for Japan's attack on Southeast Asia were to succeed, the isolationist half of the population would have to keep control of America's political process. Unfortunately, although we will never know for sure, they had a very high probability of doing this.

As we have discussed, during that period, thousands of . Americans attended rallies given by Charles Lindberg around the country who tried to keep us out of the war. Remember, as a major part of this plan, the Japanese would not attack Pearl Harbor. This would play into the hands of those who were against war at all costs. If our plan for Japan's attack on Southeast Asia were to work, the isolationist wing of both parties would need to remain in control of the American government. I believe that this would be very possible.

In addition, every week Father Coughlin preached to millions of Americans who listened to his presentations on how we should believe that the Axis powers were no threat to the U.S. if we just didn't bother them. Many of these believers were in congress and were politically powerful and very vocal.

To understand fully the attitude and effect on America, these "keep out of war at all costs" people had on the rest of us, it is best to look at the organization called, "America First Committee." It was active until the attack on Pearl Harbor when it disbanded and is said to have had 800,000 dues paying members just before the war. Its leading spokesmen were Lindberg and Father Coughlin as mentioned earlier. At his peak, it is estimated that Father Coughlin had a listening audience of 30 million Americans, more than 10% of the population.

This organization reflected German and Japanese propaganda that we should stay neutral in the Axis wars going on around the world. The members were very anti-Semitic as well and typically reflected Hitler's view that the Jews were trying to take over the world.

Their argument would have been, "they haven't attacked us and attacking them would be only to protect properties owned by Holland, France and England. This is not America's business so let's stay out of it." This attitude by powerful people would have played into Axis hands and probably kept the U. S. out of the war until the Axis decided that it would be to their advantage to attack us.

The success of our make-believe plan would be based on the assumption that the U. S. would probably not have responded to Japan's attack on Southeast Asia as they did on Japan's attack on Pearl Harbor. It is only conjecture but knowing how American felt in 1941, I believe that it is a very probable reaction. Japan would have conquered Southeast Asia easily and, possibly, Australia, China and maybe even India. For the U.S. to reconquer these lands would have been a formidable task undoubtedly costing millions of casualties on both sides. But most importantly it would have taken a resolve that probably would not have existed if Japan had not attacked the U. S. by bombing Pearl Harbor. The result of all of this is that Germany and Japan would have owned half or more of the world leaving America isolated and unable to do anything about it.

We all would be living in a totally different world today if this plan had been executed.

CHAPTER THIRTEEN

Too Close To Call

I t is easy to sit back in our easy chairs and speculate on, "what if." But there is more to this story than idle speculation. We cannot proceed without the customary thanks to the generation that saved us in spite of the America First Committee and its sympathizers. My dad was a naval officer during the war and had warned me to watch out for the isolationists in our midst in the 1930's.

Above all, thank God for President Roosevelt. He selected competent military leaders and made logical and workable plans to defeat the enemy. The only bad choice he made, in my opinion, was in promoting General Eisenhower above all other generals except Marshall, MacArthur and Arnold. General Eisenhower mostly did a good job in Europe except for some serious mistakes in the Battle of The Bulge. Some think that he was a questionable president, but that would be another book. However, both General MacArthur and General Eisenhower made blunders that will be covered later.

However, our good fortune lay in the huge mistakes that Japan and Hitler made before and during the war. Unless we think that our victory was entirely due to our brilliance, let's look at some of the stupid mistakes made by our enemies.

Germany

Hitler made a number of blunders in the war that cost Germany tens of thousands of troops and civilians. The obvious ones were Stalingrad, declaring war on the Soviet Union, bombing London instead of the British air bases, not building up his submarine force before the war started and not building long range bombers until the war was almost over. There were other less obvious blunders but let's look at arguably the worst one.

Declaring War on the United States

It is well known, as was mentioned earlier, that Japan did not alert Hitler of its intention to bomb Pearl Harbor. He was as surprised as was Roosevelt. It seems that Japan's surprise attack had a different effect on Hitler. Initially he couldn't decide whether to follow up with an attack of his own or ignore us. The logic of doing nothing was overwhelming. He knew that a large number of Americans were against fighting Germany even after Pearl Harbor as we discussed in Chapter 1. No one knows what Hitler was thinking about during the four days after the Pearl Harbor attack, and we can only guess.

There is no question but that he was still angry about American's contribution to Germany's defeat in WW I. Our contribution to the Allied victory in 1918 was significant and he hated us for it. He also saw the damage that Japan did to our Pacific Fleet and decided that we would be a pushover so he wanted in on the action. There was also the fact that the Axis powers had a mutual defense agreement that provided that if any of the Axis powers was attacked, the others would join in and fight with their attacked partner. This does not account for his declaration of war on the United States four days after Pearl Harbor because Japan was not attacked, they did the attacking.

The most important fact that he was probably considering was the issue raised in Chapter one, that most Americans would not support a war against Germany. He probably assumed that we would surrender the minute he declared war. Here is another example of not knowing your enemy and paying dearly for your stupidity.

It is not known what exactly caused Hitler to do it, but four days after the Japanese attack on Pearl Harbor, Germany declared war on the United States. Now our antiwar sentiment dissipated and all Americans joined together to defeat all of the Axis nations. Hitler had learned nothing from WW I and Germany paid an enormous price for his stupid blunder.

Japan

West Coast. The attack on Pearl Harbor and the failure of Admiral Nagumo to order a second strike has been discussed. The failure of Admiral Yamamoto to have his strike force of six carriers continue on to the west coast of the U.S. cost Japan the war. All of the military and industrial bases and war plants that we had in California, Oregon and Washington could have been destroyed in an attack that never came.

The Panama Canal. Why Japan didn't execute a coordinated attack on the Panama Canal in December of 1941 has never been fully explained. It would have been easy sine the canal was lightly guarded and its destruction would have kept the ships of the Atlantic Fleet out of the Pacific for months maybe even years.

Guadalcanal. The Japanese realized early in the war of the strategic importance of Guadalcanal in the Solomon Islands. They began building an airfield on it that would allow their medium range bombers to attack our shipping lanes and destroy convoys headed to Australia.

The Japanese, however, failed to anticipate the fact that American forces would also recognize the importance of the island and did not man it with adequate forces to protect it from invasion. It was invaded by U.S. Marines in August 1942 and fell into our hands completely by January 1943. Their failure to provide sufficient defense for the island until well after our marines had landed allowed the U.S. to begin its island hopping campaign to Japan.

First Battle of Savo Island. The American invasion fleet had landed a Marine force on the beaches of Guadalcanal during the first week in

August 1942. The ships were still unloading troops and supplies on the third night of the invasion when a Japanese cruiser force commanded by Japanese Admiral Mikawa steamed down the Straights known as the Slot with the intent of sinking the American invasion ships.

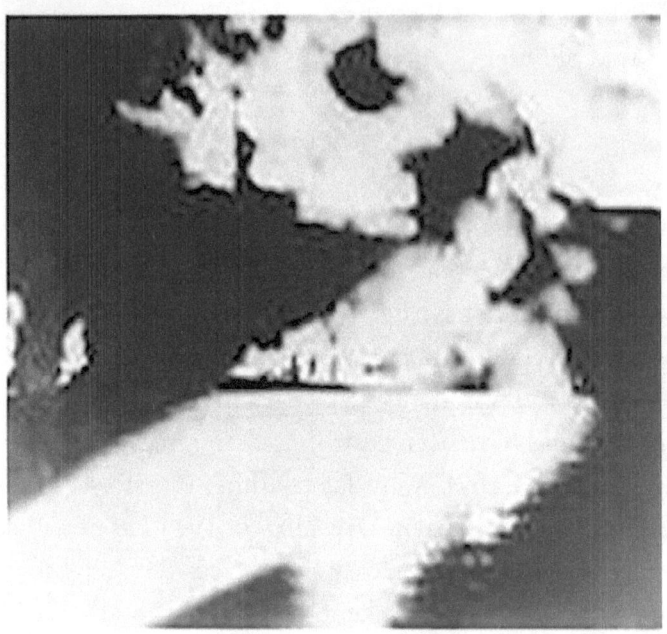

American cruiser USS Quincy being sunk at Savo Island

Five Allied heavy cruisers blocked their path to the unloading supply ships under command of a British Admiral Crutchley. Unfortunately, Admiral Crutchley on board the Australian cruiser Canberra decided to go ashore to confer with the marine general. When he left his fleet, he forgot to tell the ship's captains or designate a person in charge in his absence.

That night the Japanese strike force arrived in the midst of the allied ships and opened fire on them all. The Allied ships awaited orders from the Allied admiral, which never came. Consequently, four of the cruisers, the Canberra, Astoria, Vincennes and Quincy were sunk. Only the Chicago survived.

Vice Admiral Mikawa IJN

Japanese Admiral Mikawa's force was then unopposed in its primary mission to destroy the invasion transports and auxiliary ships unloading at the beach. He could have wiped out several dozen lightly armed ships and their crews. Instead of taking up on this unique opportunity, Mikawa decided to turn north and return to his base leaving the American auxiliary ships unharmed. Admiral Yamamoto was furious and immediately relieved Mikawa of his command.

It is difficult to measure the cost of Mikawa's reluctance to press his advantage after sinking four escorting allied cruisers. Our auxiliary ships unloading troops and cargo on the beaches of Guadalcanal were pretty much all we had of this type of ship in the Pacific at the time.

Their loss would have doomed the marines on the beach and ended the possibility of any further invasion of Japanese islands for many months and would have kept Guadalcanal in Japanese hands. The Battle of Savo Island must rank as one of Japan's biggest blunders during the war.

The Battle of Komandorski Straight. This battle took place in the straight of water between the western end of the Aleutian Islands and the eastern edge of Russia in March of 1943. A small American task force of two cruisers, the Salt Lake City and Richmond and four destroyers under command of Admiral McMorris were patrolling the area to keep the Japanese forces out of the Aleutians.

They were suddenly faced with a larger Japanese force of four cruisers, five destroyers and two troop transports under command of Admiral Hosogaya. The Japanese intended to invade one of the islands in the Aleutians with the troops on the two transports. The Japanese force joined into a battle formation and steamed toward the smaller American force. Both sides opened up and the battle was severe as both sides scored hits. Unfortunately, the American ships were getting the worst of it as the superior Japanese force took control of the battle.

Soon the Salt Lake City took hits in its engine room and finally stopped dead in the water as the Japanese ships continued to pound it. Admiral McMorris on board the USS Richmond continued to fight to try to save the Salt Lake City, but it was becoming hopeless.

Suddenly, and for reasons never fully explained by Admiral Hosogaya, he turned his squadron away from the American ships and headed home while sinking none of the American ships that his force had badly damaged.

The Japanese gave up the fight at the moment of victory and the battle was won by a smaller badly damaged American fleet that now controlled the western tip of the Aleutians. This tactical blunder by another Japanese admiral may have cost the Japanese control of the Aleutian Islands for the rest of the war.

USS Richmond, Flagship Alaska Fleet My dad's ship in 1923-25

Battle of Leyte Gulf. The battle of Leyte Gulf consisted of four separate sea battles between major Japanese and American naval forces in the summer of 1944. The major Japanese blunder occurred in the battle called The Battle Off Samar Island and it included a major blunder by the American Admiral "Bull" Halsey that will be covered later.

USS Salt Lake City.

The American invasion fleet, under Admiral Sprague was offloading troops and supplies at Leyte beaches while being protected by a small fleet consisting of three escort carriers and their support destroyers.

Admiral Halsey and his Third Fleet were supposed to be standing by to protect the invasion forces from attack by a large Japanese attack force that was expected to arrive shortly.

Unfortunately, Admiral Halsey decided to pursue a decoy Japanese naval force far to the north leaving the invasion fleet unprotected. Suddenly, a large Japanese task force under Admiral Kurita and consisting of four battleships including the mammoth Yamato, eight cruisers and eleven destroyers steamed down from the north and into the middle of Admiral Sprague's tiny invasion force. The stage was set for a massacre of thousands of American soldiers and sailors.

Admiral Sprague's tiny force fought gallantly sinking or disabling three Japanese cruisers. The American force lost two escort carriers, two destroyers and a destroyer escort in the exchange of gunfire. The airplanes from the carriers were not equipped to sink battleships, but they hit them with all they had.

The giant Japanese battleships were poised to continue south into the middle of the troop and auxiliary ships and wipe them out when Admiral Kurita decided to turn tail and head for home. He had killed over a thousand American sailors and sank five of our ships, but he could have decimated the entire invasion fleet at Leyte when he decided to go home.

His blunder was not entirely caused by his stupidity. He did not have air cover nor sufficient intelligence to tell him the size of the American force he was facing. The northern decoy Japanese force had failed to notify him that Halsey's Third Fleet had taken the bait and he thought he was facing America's battleships and fleet carriers. He mistook Admiral Sprague's tiny force for Admiral Halsey's massive fleet and retired to protect his remaining battleships.

Nevertheless, history will not treat Admiral Kurita kindly. He turned and fled in the face of an inferior force when, with a little initiative, he could have destroyed America's invasion of the Philippines in one battle. This was one of the greatest blunders of the Pacific war.

These four blunders by Japanese naval forces, together, resulted in the defeat of Japan and saved thousands of American lives. It is interesting that all four were caused by admirals who were not able to bring their fleets into a winning engagement even though they all had big advantages. We Americans need to give the four Japanese admirals a vote of thanks.

United States

The U.S. had its share of stupid blunders during the war, but most were kept secret from the population for propaganda and morale reasons. The first one was present in 1941 and almost cost us the battle of the Pacific.

Submarine Torpedoes. The Mark 14 submarine torpedo was without a doubt the worst designed weapon on either side in World War II. It had several major problems: it travelled at ten to twelve feet lower in the water than set, it didn't always explode on contact with enemy ships, it didn't always explode by the magnetic trigger, it often exploded halfway to the target, it would change course, turn 180 degrees and come back and sink the submarine that fired it.

There were many instances of one or more of these events occurring during the first twenty-one months of the war when the most effective operational warships we had were submarines. These malfunctions were duly reported to the submarine commander at Pearl Harbor who was very skeptical at first. The sub skippers were accused of being poor shots and making up excuses for their misses. But the malfunctions happened so often that the Pacific sub commander, Admiral Lockwood, finally had to admit that something was wrong with the torpedoes. He finally reported the malfunctions to the Bureau of Ordnance (BuOrd) in Washington and the torpedo station in Rhode Island that had built all of the navy's torpedoes. The officer in charge of BuOrd, Admiral William Blandy, accused Admiral Lockwood and his submariners of incompetence and refused to do anything about the malfunctioning torpedoes. The problems were caused by lack of testing and were easily fixable had there been a capable Admiral in charge of the Board.

Mark XIV Torpedo being loaded onto a submarine

The failure to fix or even address the problem caused the death of hundreds of our sailors and the sinking of many of our submarines. It didn't get fixed until the navy's head officer, Admiral King, came down hard on Admiral Blandy and forced him to address the problem in 1943.

Blandy should have been stood up against the wall and shot for his gross incompetence and stupid ego. Instead the Navy promoted him to Commander, Joint Task Force One, then to Commander, Destroyers Pacific Fleet and finally to Commander in Charge, Atlantic Fleet. He was a full, four star admiral when he retired in 1950. As an ex-navy officer, I can testify with personal knowledge that our navy sometimes does stupid things. This one almost cost us the war. It is interesting to note that the American public was not told of this fiasco until after the war ended.

Battle of The Philippines. Early in the morning of December 8, 1941 Philippines time (Dec 7th Hawaii time), General MacArthur was told of the Japanese attack on Pearl Harbor and warned to be prepared for an imminent Japanese attack on the Philippines. The officer in charge of his air force, General Brereton, immediately asked General MacArthur, through his chief of staff, to allow him to launch his airplanes so they wouldn't be caught on the ground.

Unfortunately, MacArthur refused permission and the entire American air force in the Philippines was wiped out while sitting on the ground in one Japanese air raid. MacArthur never explained the reason for his monumental blunder, a blunder that went a long way to our eventual defeat in the Philippines. The popular MacArthur was never held to account for his stupid decision and the American public were not made aware of it until after the war.

There is an alternate story that MacArthur sent all his planes up when he heard about the Pearl Harbor attack, but the Japanese attack force was delayed by bad weather. The American airplanes all ran out of gas at the same time and had to return to base together to get refueled. The Japanese then attacked and destroyed them all on the ground. Whichever account is true, we lost all of our planes that MacArthur could have saved with good planning.

Battle of Midway. The battle of Midway is covered in Chapter 16 and is considered to be the most important American victory in 1942. Admiral Spruance's fleet sank four major Japanese aircraft carriers in two days of aerial combat in June. So why am I listing it as a major American mistake?

I call the readers' attention to the Battle of Gettysburg in the Civil War in July of 1863. After the great Union Army victory, Union General Meade refused to send his troops in pursuit of Confederate General Lee as his army retreated into Virginia. President Lincoln was furious with General Meade for not destroying General Lee's wounded army on its retreat south. In fact, the President had Meade fired and brought in General Grant.

How does this relate to the Battle of Midway in June of 1942? On the second day of the battle all of the Japanese carriers had been sunk and their huge fleet had no air cover. Spruance still had two aircraft carriers operational and ready for battle, but Spruance ordered the fleet to return to Pearl Harbor and let the Japanese fleet return home with no more losses. One can only speculate on the damage Spruance's aircraft could have done to the remaining Japanese warships had he chosen to follow them home. He had a week of unopposed air attacks possible on unprotected surface ships, but he decided to go home.

Apologists for Admiral Spruance claim that his fleet was in no shape to pursue the Japanese to Japan, but I disagree. Victory goes to the bold.

I have never heard any official criticism of Admiral Spruance for his decision to break off action and come home with enemy ships still within range, but I think it was a significant American blunder.

Battle of Leyte Gulf. The battle of Leyte Gulf was discussed earlier in the section on Japanese blunders. Admiral Halsey also committed a massive blunder that cost our navy the lives of several thousand sailors.

His Third Fleet was given the responsibility of protecting the landing force made up of escort carriers, destroyers and many auxiliaries. However, he detected a large Japanese carrier force north of him and he directed his ships away from the gulf and to steam north to attack the decoy enemy force.

He was able to sink the decoy force but while he was away, a strong Japanese task force that he thought had been destroyed steamed unopposed onto the area around Leyte and sank several American aircraft carriers and destroyers unopposed by Halsey.

Admiral Halsey has been heavily criticized for his actions in that battle, and, although he had reasons that he thought were plausible for his actions, history has not been supportive of his decisions in the battle and I agree. He had battleships in his force that were of no use in his run northward that he could have left to protect the beaches and the landing craft but he took them with him leaving the landing ships at the mercy of the Yamato and her friends. Halsey deserves all of the criticism that he has received over the years.

Admiral "Bull" Halsey

German Submarine Warfare in The Atlantic. When the war with Germany broke out four days after the Japanese attack on Pearl Harbor, their submarine fleet was immediately active along our east coast. Ships steaming up and down the Atlantic coast were silhouetted at night against the lights from the casinos along the New Jersey shore. The government asked the casinos to shut off their exterior lights for the duration but casino owners refused saying that to do so would cut into their profits. Consequently, hundreds of American sailors were killed as more and more ships were torpedoed along the coast.

After months of this useless slaughter, the government finally forced the casinos to shut off their lights and the sinking of ships along the coast dropped off.

Another navy blunder happened during the early months of the war in the Atlantic. The navy was initially short of antisubmarine patrol boats. Consequently the New York Yacht Club offered to use its boats to patrol the east coast and alert the Navy when they spotted submarines. Unfortunately, the Navy said that patrolling the coast was their job and declined the generous offer. But since they had an inadequate number of patrol craft to do the job, many ships were sunk that were lost unnecessarily due to their stupidity.

Attack on Pearl Harbor. The blunders made by both the Army and the Navy prior to the Japanese attack have been outlined in previous chapters so they won't be restated here. However, there is one precaution they could have taken that is so obvious it defies belief.

The Navy patrol craft took off every morning at exactly 8:00 AM without fail. Japanese saboteurs told Tokyo of this habit and the attacking force naturally arrived at their target just before 8:00 AM undetected. If the navy had varied their patrol searches starting at say 6:00 AM the Japanese fleet might have been detected.

The army and navy commanders were equally responsible for not preparing for an attack as was outlined previously. General Short and Admiral Kimmel were duly relieved of duty and lowered in rank but neither was court martialed.

Much has been written since 1941 trying to shift the blame for our lack of preparedness on the president and away from the two commanders. It is all stupid speculation mostly made by people who hated President Roosevelt.

My dad's ship was stationed at Pearl Harbor in 1924-25 and he told me after the pearl Harbor attack that there were navy fighter planes patrolling the sky over head of the fleet every day. As an ex-naval officer, I will state again that the commanding officer of any military unit is ultimately responsible for the safety of his/her ship or unit. There are no excuses.

The Sinking of HMS Repulse and Prince of Wales. Just before the Pearl Harbor attack the British sent two of their largest warships to Singapore. The Repulse and the Prince of Wales were intended to support the U.S. Navy's Asiatic Fleet and repulse Japan's planned attack on Malaysia. The ships were docked at Singapore when Japan attacked and two days after the attack on Pearl Harbor, wisely put to sea to meet whatever Japanese fleet may be headed their way. Before they left Singapore, the RAF offered to keep Spitfires overhead to protect the two ships from enemy aircraft attack. Unfortunately, Admiral Phillips, the commander of the task force, declined the offer saying that air cover would not be necessary.

Two days later the Japanese air force located the British task force and easily sank the two ships. The Allies were no longer able to provide any defense of the East Indies, Malaysia or Singapore. The gross stupidity of British Admiral Phillips not only cost the Allies the use of two important capital ships in the Pacific but also certainly hastened the fall of South East Asia. Fortunately, the admiral went down with his ship.

The Battle of Anzio Beach in Italy. In early 1944 General Mark Clark appointed General John Lucas to be in charge of an amphibious landing in an area north of the existing battle lines called Anzio Beach. It was a brilliant plan that depended on surprise and swiftness of movement.

The American and British forces landed unopposed taking the Germans completely by surprise. General Lukas marched his men inland and then brought them to a halt. They were surrounded by mountains on all sides and hemmed in by marshlands on their front and rear.

Royal Navy's HMS Prince of Wales sunk near Singapore

The Germans quickly responded and formed on the mountains around the stalled Allied Army. General Lucas kept his Army still when it should have been moving rapidly inland giving the Germans time to mount a serious counter attack.

For several months the Germans pounded the helpless Allied forces from the surrounding mountain tops while they flooded the marshland around the trapped Allies.

Finally, in May, General Clarke relieved General Lucas of his command and replaced him with General Truscott who finally led the decimated Allies out and drove the German troops away. Anzio was a monumental blunder by General Lucas that cost the Allies thousands of unnecessary casualties.

The Battle of The Bulge. In November and December of 1944, the German Wehrmacht accomplished a brilliant build up and execution of a massive attack through the Ardennes Forest in Belgium. They pushed the unprepared American 7th Army back into Belgium before we recouped and pushed the Germans back into Germany with the help of Patton's 3rd Army, but not before losing tens of thousands Of American soldiers.

General Eisenhower claimed that he knew nothing about the German buildup as he allowed his troops to be spread out so thin that they were no match for the Wehrmacht. Consequently, we took enormous casualties. He claimed that all of the German prisoners taken before the attack said that the German Army was decimated and had been badly defeated in their retreat across France. Eisenhower bought this lie hook, line and sinker.

We have known for a while that the British Intelligence (MI6) had broken the secret German code and were eavesdropping into German conversations for most of the war. After the war, the British said that they had warned General Eisenhower that in November of 1944 they had detected increased radio traffic among German Army units stationed in and around the Ardennes. They heard no direct mention of an imminent attack, but warned Eisenhower that increased radio traffic usually meant that an attack was being planned.

General Eisenhower chose to ignore the MI6 input saying that his intelligence, based on German prisoner reports, was that no attack was being planned. It is interesting to note that when Eisenhower became president, he asked the British not to announce that they had broken the German code until after his death, which they did. Why would Eisenhower not want the fact that the British had broken the German code be released until long after the end of the war? Could we have suspected that he had been warned of the German activity in the Ardennes that he ignored?

General Dwight D. Eisenhower

Whether or not the British had warned him, there was no excuse for Eisenhower not sending out patrols on reconnaissance missions to find out exactly what was the German troop disposition. Whether it's army or navy, nothing equals knowing what the enemy is up to and what is the size of his force.

Nothing can be proven at this time in history but it should be remembered that a blunder occurred at the highest European Army command in the winter of 1944 and the commanding officer is responsible (See Pearl Harbor in previous chapters) Eisenhower had never been asked to explain why he took the input from German POW's above intelligence from MI6 that cost thousands of American lives.

This ends the segment on major blunders that had an effect or could have had a serious effect on the outcome of the war. There were blunders of less consequence that are too numerous to mention and that have been covered in other books. Suffice to say that the Allies were extremely lucky first of all that the mistakes we made were not terminal and that the mistakes made by the Axis powers were.

Many mistakes are made in wartime and most are caused by lack of intelligence. The ones listed in this chapter are those major blunders for which there was adequate intelligence or good judgment to prevent them.

We were lucky. We lost tens of thousands of men that was not necessary and we could have lost the war if the Wehrmacht had stored up enough gasoline before their attack through the Ardennes.

CHAPTER FOURTEEN

Why We Won And They Lost

A professor whose name I have forgotten, who was my teacher in my master's degree program at San Jose State University was obsessed with statistics and war. He felt that something could be learned by plotting mathematic variables relating to war activities. His favorite graph was a plot on semi- log paper of the casualties of a war as a function of time into it. On his plot, the x-axis was linear and the Y-axis was the logarithm of the number of deaths.

He had gone back into history at every war for which there was data and plotted the years into the war on the x axis and the log of the total casualties along the y axis. He showed us that the shape of the resulting curves was the same for every war although the numbers were different. Of particular interest was his conclusion that almost every war ended at the same spot on the curve. He could predict when every war ended with great accuracy.

He had plotted World War II as two separate wars, one against Germany and the other against Japan. The war against Germany ended right on time, statistically. However, he showed us that the war against Japan had ended much sooner than it should have according to his numbers. He showed us that the war against Japan should have extended into 1946 maybe 1947, but it ended in August of 1945. What caused that? We all know what happened in Hiroshima and Nagasaki.

This professor's work proved statistically beyond any doubt that the bombs did stop the war prematurely saving hundreds of thousands of casualties on both sides. It is strange that this conclusion is controversial today because it was so obvious to those of us who were alive in that summer. Let's take a look at the facts as we know them today.

The argument has been made by people who were not alive then or who had an axe to grind or who were just plain out of touch with reality that the Japanese were beaten and were ready to surrender at the time and the bombs did not need to be dropped. Let's look at this argument as it is presented.

First of all, the Japanese had never been beaten in a war and never considered themselves beaten before the bombs were dropped in 1945. People who believe this state that there were Japanese "colonels" who were putting out feelers for Japan to surrender if we would allow them to keep their emperor. It is true that this happened but it is also true that the Japanese government disowned them and said that the colonels did not speak for the emperor.

Before going any further we need to remember that the official position of the United States was that we would accept nothing short of "unconditional surrender." So, the offer of the colonels, even if official, would not have been acceptable to the United States.

It was also stated, mostly by our Navy, that our submarines had cut off all shipping to Japan and they were starving to death and would have surrendered at any moment. This argument misses one very important point.

There were between 30,000 and 90,000 Allied prisoners of war living in POW camps in Japan and depending on Japan's supply of food to survive. When the war actually ended and we released all the prisoners, it was found by our medical people that our prisoners would have survived average of thirty days if the war had continued. So, the people who make this argument are willing to have given up the lives of tens of thousands of Americans POW's to save a few thousand Japanese civilians. I guarantee that no one in the U.S. in 1945 would have agreed with this position.

It must be remembered that even after the two bombs were dropped, the Japanese Diet (ruling cabinet) voted against surrendering. It wasn't until the emperor asked them to reconsider their vote that they voted to surrender. Even after they finally voted to surrender at the emperor's request, the Japanese army attempted to continue the war.

It was found after the war that the Japanese military had fully intended to fight on the beaches and in their homes to the last person, if necessary, rather than surrender. Fortunately, the emperor thought that we had more atomic bombs and were willing to use them to destroy Japanese cities. Actually, we had used up all we had and it would take several months to build more if Japan had not surrendered.

There is no doubt among thinking people that the atomic bombs ended the worst war in world history and saved hundreds of thousands of lives. Yes, it cost hundreds of thousands of lives, but so did the fire-bombing of Tokyo in the spring of 1945.

Without the bombs, fighting would have continued for one to two years with American forces fighting hand to hand across Japan. Japan, by their own admission, would never have surrendered but would have fought to the last death. If it were not for the bomb, and President Truman's willingness to use it, there would be no Japan as we know it today.

One last point is the possibility that part of Truman's reason for using the bomb was to show the world, especially the Russians, what an atomic bomb would do to a city and its people. We will never know if this is true but no country has dared to use an atomic weapon since 1945. Whether President Truman intended it or not, the entire world knows what destruction an atomic or hydrogen bomb can do.

Atomic Bomb

CHAPTER FIFTEEN

Only Good News For The Public

We survived World War II mostly with the public not knowing how close we came to disaster. In the Pacific, the Japanese cabinet and a half dozen Japanese admirals made the difference between Japan's success and their ultimate defeat. As mentioned earlier, they had superior equipment and forces at the war's beginning and if they had been used properly, Japan would probably have prevailed against us at least in the short term. Some Allied military leaders made equally bad blunders, but the American public typically knew nothing about them and we were able to recover.

I can remember in 1943 a friend of my dad's who was in the navy serving on a minesweeper, told us about how we lost the four heavy cruisers in the battle of Savo Island the year before. He was shocked when my dad replied that the American public had been told nothing about it. I don't recall that we were ever told about the sinking of the Quincy, Canberra, Astoria and Vincennes until after the war had ended. The public was absolutely never told about the sinking of the USS Juneau and the loss of the five Sullivan brothers on it, nor the loss of the USS Indianapolis during the last week of the war. We were given nothing but good news.

The story of Colin Kelly was a textbook example of propaganda that was fed to us to keep our spirits up. It seems that in the battle of the Philippines in 1941, 42, Kelly, the pilot of a B-17, dove his plane into the Japanese battleship Haruna sinking it on the spot. The fact was that his plane had dropped bombs on a heavy cruiser lightly damaging it and he was shot down by Japanese planes while returning to his base. The Haruna was sunk at anchor in Kure naval base in July of 1945, but Kelly is still considered to be an American hero.

In summary, in 1941 the United States was outclassed by the Axis in almost every weapon:

- Torpedoes (Japan)
- Fighter planes (Germany and Japan)
- Tanks and machine guns (Germany)
- Number of aircraft carriers (Japan)
- Field artillery (Germany)
- Size and age of our Pacific Fleet (Japan)
- Training and tactics (Japan)
- Preparations for war (Japan)

Fortunately, the American public was unaware of most of these and we immediately went to work to build the greatest fighting force ever seen. It took time, but was an amazing turn around whose success was not always obvious to those who knew the whole story.

CHAPTER SIXTEEN

The Allies Did Some Things Right

I n spite of the mistakes we made and the bad things that happened to us, we made several wise moves, created great inventions and had some good luck along the way. Let's begin with Doolittle's raid on Tokyo in the spring of 1942.

Doolittle's Raid on Tokyo

When the fleet with Doolittle's planes on board was steaming west to bomb Japan, they were one day away from launching their planes off the Japanese coast when the fleet came upon several Japanese fishing boats. The fishing boats radioed to Tokyo that an American fleet with aircraft carriers was approaching Japan, and they gave out the location before they were all sunk by naval gunfire. Now the Japanese air force knew that our carriers were out there and correctly surmised our intentions. However, they made a big mistake, but one that any country would have made.

The two aircraft carriers, the Hornet and the Enterprise normally carried Navy single engine dive bombers and torpedo bombers. The Japanese knew this and, knowing their range, calculated that to make a round trip bombing run and return to the carriers, these navy planes would need to be one day closer to Japan before their planes were launched. So, they decided to wait a day then put up a massive curtain of fighter planes and shoot down all the American dive bombers before they reached Japan. This was a good idea except that Colonel Doolittle and his men weren't flying Navy dive bombers, they were flying Air Corps twin-engine B-25 medium bombers.

The reader needs to understand the significance of this situation. Never before in the history of aviation had a twin engine bomber taken off from an aircraft carrier, and no one on either side believed it was possible. It was not possible to land such a big plane on a carrier, but Colonel Doolittle believed that, with a little practice, a few bombers could make it off the flight deck of the Hornet when it was going full speed into the wind.

In that part of the world there is often at least fifteen knots of wind blowing, so the Hornet would turn into the wind and increase to flank speed of about thirty to thirty-five knots. Then the planes would be fifty knots toward take off speed before they began to move.

The colonel and his men talked it over and decided to take off a day early to surprise the Japanese before they were ready. Amazingly, it worked! The Japanese interceptor pilots were enjoying a glass of sake that day, and no one believed that the explosions they heard were from American bombers. The American pilots were in and out of Japan before the Japanese could believe what was happening.

Because they couldn't land on the carriers, the planes continued flying westerly ending up in China. Most of the crews were saved, allowing them to return to America and fight again. The Chinese people paid dearly for helping the American flyers, many thousands were tortured and killed by Japanese soldiers in retaliation for helping the Americans.

The aircrews were treated as heroes back home and Lt. Colonel Doolittle was promoted by President Roosevelt over the rank of colonel to the rank of brigadier general. The success of this mission was due to a combination of good planning, good decision making, good execution, bad decision making by the Japanese and just plain good luck.

The Battle of Midway Island

Many good books and movies have been written and made about the sea battle that occurred at Midway during the first week of June, 1942, so we won't cover all of the details of the battle and its preparation here. The U.S. Navy made several excellent moves and some lucky ones to win the battle. In addition, we made a serious blunder, in my opinion, that cost us dearly during the rest of the war. The blunder is discussed in Chapter 13.

Admiral Yamamoto felt that it was necessary to occupy Midway and use it as a base from which the IJN would warn Japan of any American movement west across the Pacific. Consequently, they threw everything they had into the battle including their four operational aircraft carriers. The Admiral would have put six into the battle, but one had been sunk and one damaged, both in the battle of the Coral Sea a month earlier.

Here is where LCDR Rochefort and his code breakers saved the day. He correctly predicted the date and location of the attack based on his code breaking. Admiral Nimitz deployed our three remaining aircraft carriers, the Hornet, Enterprise and the damaged Yorktown and their escorts and ordered them to steam from Pearl Harbor to a position northeast of Midway that would allow them to intercept the Japanese fleet as it attacked Midway.

On June 4th, Japanese planes began attacking Midway and searching for the American fleet that they believed was out there somewhere waiting for them. American carrier planes were sent out to search for the enemy fleet, and here luck entered into the fight.

One group of dive bombers from the Yorktown headed due west, found nothing and returned to their carrier empty handed. They were sent in this direction by orders from Admiral Fletcher who never explained why he sent them in that direction when intelligence indicated that the Japanese fleet was southwest of the American fleet. Fortunately, the planes from the Hornet and the Enterprise had better luck.

As they were flying southwest, their fuel was running low, and they still had not found the Japanese fleet. Suddenly they spotted a Japanese cruiser headed northwest from Midway and toward what the American pilots assumed was the enemy fleet. So, they turned northwest and watched their fuel supply get dangerously low. Soon they were rewarded when they spotted the Japanese fleet dead ahead.

The torpedo bomber flight, Squadron #8, led the attack as they flew down to sea level and dropped all their torpedoes. Unfortunately, all their torpedoes missed and the entire squadron was shot down by Japanese fighters. All of the pilots were killed except one. Ensign Gay survived and was rescued by an American float plane after the battle ended.

The torpedo bomber attack would be considered a failure except that it diverted all the Japanese fighters down to sea level and left the high altitude undefended, where the deadly attack originated.

American dive bombers fell out of the sky dropping 500-pound bombs in the midst of fueling Japanese planes into the lower decks of the carriers. Three of the enemy aircraft carriers were sunk immediately, and the fourth one was sunk the following day. It was an enormous American victory except for one thing.

At the end of the battle, the IJN had many large surface ships remaining at Midway but no aircraft carriers. Th at means that the Japanese ships had no air cover. Their remaining ships were completely vulnerable to air attack, while we had two aircraft carriers undamaged and ready for a fight. However, Admiral Spruance ordered his fleet to turn around and head back to Pearl Harbor. His retreat allowed many large Japanese warships to escape back to Japan to fight another day. This issue is covered more completely in Chapter 13.

The Dummy Allied Army

As the Allies were preparing to cross the English Channel and invade France in 1944, it became obvious that we could gain considerable advantage over Hitler and his troops if we could convince him that our landings would take place away from the actual landing beaches. So, work began on one of the most deceptive ploys ever executed in wartime.

It began with the loudly proclaimed appointment of American General George Patton to head the fictitious Third Army. Hitler knew that General Patton was the best field general in our Army, and that wherever he was stationed in England would likely be close to the French landing beach. So, with big fanfare, General Patton and his staff set up training operations in England directly across the channel from the French town of Calais. Although the Third Army consisted only of General Patton and his staff, the British built fake tanks out of rubber that looked real and set them up around Patton's "headquarters." The British captured several German spies and "turned" them making them radio Hitler that the Allies intended to land on the French Beach near Calais, several hundred miles from the actual intended landing spot in Normandy.

This fakery carried over to the invasion itself because Hitler believed that the landing at Normandie was a diversion only and that the real landing would be on the beach near Calais. As a result of this belief, he refused to commit his Panzer tank division against the Allied troops on Normandy beaches until they had pushed considerably inland beyond the beachhead.

This brilliant bit of deception by the Allies and Hitler's accompanying buy in saved probably hundreds, maybe thousands, of Allied casualties, and allowed us to retake Paris that summer of 1944. The actual Third Army was created in France several weeks after the invasion with General Patton in charge.

Design of The Spitfire

When England and Germany went to war in 1939, the British Spitfire fighter plane and its German nemesis, the ME-109, were pretty close to one another in speed, maneuverability and climb rate. Maybe the Spitfire was slightly ahead, but not by a big amount. Both sides worked to improve their designs but neither side made much of an improvement until the British engine designers came up with a brilliant idea. Why not get more power out of their Merlin engine by increasing its compression ratio?

It was an excellent idea, but increasing the engine's compression ratio would require 100 octane gasoline, and no refinery in the world could make 100 octane gasoline at that time. The Rolls Royce Merlin engine was, and is, the best internal combustion engine in the world, so their engineers put down their slide rules, put on their suits and went to visit the Royal Dutch oil refinery. Fortunately, the Manager of The Aviation Division of the refinery was the one man in the world who would understand their quandary. He was James Doolittle, the same man who would lead the successful air raid on Tokyo in 1942.

He was the first person in the world to earn a PhD in aeronautical engineering in the early 1920's. He immediately understood what the Rolls Royce engineers were trying to accomplish and said he would do what he could. He called a meeting of the company's board of directors, explained the problem and requested that they expand their refining capability to make 100 octane aviation fuel. The investment to accomplish this was huge, but the need was so great that the board authorized the spending of several million dollars to expand their refinery.

Shortly, the Luftwaffe pilots began to notice that they were being out-maneuvered and more easily shot down. They finally downed a Spitfire over France, removed the engine and tore it apart. They soon saw the reason for the change. The Spitfire had a compression ratio of over nine to one which could only be accomplished with 100 octane aviation fuel. The Germans did not have access to modern refining so there was no way they could keep up. The British won that round.

The P-51 Mustang

The American P-51 fighter plane was unquestionably the finest fighter plane in WW II and is credited with winning the war in Europe almost single handedly. The story of its design is some-what controversial, but it will be presented here as the author understands it.

The story begins with the American long range bombers, the B-17 and B-24, developed in the late 1930's. Before we entered the war, the Air Corps was bragging that their new bombers did not need fighter escort, because they could get to the target and return to base without difficulty. This was due to the large number of machine guns in the bombers which could shoot down enemy fighter planes easily without getting shot down themselves. The B-17, for example, had ten .50 caliber machine guns for its defense. Surely no fighter plane could penetrate that fire power!

As a consequence, the fighter planes built during that period, the P-38, P-40, and P 47, did not have the range to escort the bombers all the way from England to Berlin and back. They would escort the bombers as far as the Dutch coast and then turn back and let the B-17's continue on to Berlin without escort. This fiasco cost the lives of thousands of American airmen and made the bombing of Germany very expensive in high casualties and lost aircraft.

The problem was that the fighter planes had a wing design called by engineers a "turbulent wing." That meant that its design caused turbulence over the top of the wing resulting in high drag on the plane. This drag resulted in high gasoline consumption and shorter range, but it was the standard design for Allied fighter planes at the beginning of the war.

Early in the war, British Aircraft designers decided to design the best fighter plane in the world by combining the best elements of all planes, enemy and allied. When they completed their design, they first went to British aircraft plants but were told that all the manufacturing was maxed out building existing aircraft. No one in Britain could build another airplane, so the British designers took their plans to the United States and visited the aircraft plants to see if anyone had room for another plane. They met with rejection at Lockheed, Grumman, Douglas, Republic, Curtiss, Boeing, and Consolidated. No one had any room to build another fighter plane until they reached North American in Los Angeles. They happily agreed to build the new plane for Britain and began by making enough small changes to the design to call it their own.

In a few months, the first new fighter came off the assembly line, and an Air Corps test pilot was called in to see how it flew. After a couple of hours in the air, he landed and jumped out of the plane with excitement saying that this was the best fighter plane he had ever flown, and it could rule the skies, except for one problem. The engine was inadequate. The Allison V-12 engine made by General Motors was under powered and did not have a turbo charger that would make the new plane able to compete against the ME-109 at high altitude.

Fortunately, The Rolls Royce Merlin engine was being made in the U. S. by Packard Motor Company, and it was immediately substituted for the Allison, much to GM's disgust, and the new fighter was not given to England but became the P-51, the workhorse in the U.S. Army Air Corps.

Its wings had a laminar flow design that reduced the drag on the plane, and with drop off fuel tanks, allowed it to escort bombers all the way to Berlin and back. It is reported that when Hermann Goering, the head of the German Luftwaffe, first saw the P-51 flying over Berlin, he remarked that the war was now lost. His remark came true in the early summer of 1945.

The beauty of the P-51 was not just in its wing design, but that its entire body was designed with low drag compared to other fighters. The British designers were the best in the world, and they were disappointed that their new plane was coopted by the United States. However, they accepted the fact that only the United States had the manufacturing capability to build a new fighter that became the workhorse of the air fight over Europe.

North American Aviation gave the award for their design of the P-51 to their star aerospace engineer, Edgar Schmued and it is said that his design was based on requirements given to him by the British government. Who actually designed the P-51 depends on your definition of "design" but probably engineers in both countries contributed to the final configuration.

The P-51 gave the Allies the control of the skies, and that was important. It is interesting to note that North American Aviation claims to this day that it designed the P-51. They certainly contributed to the design, and the laminar flow wing became an essential part of future jet fighters that they built. As Goering correctly said when P-51 flew over Berlin, the war was lost because of the new fighter that the British had designed, the Americans had built, and US pilots had flown.

Critical Spying

There were many stories of spying by the Allies during the war that made a critical difference at important times in the fighting. One true story of a Soviet spy tops the list of important spy events that shaped the outcome of the war.

A German industrialist who was actually a Soviet spy was living in Tokyo. His father was German and his mother Russian, but his sympathies lay with the Soviet Union. He had given Stalin some news on the Japanese and German troop movements during the 1930s but most were ignored.

As 1941 was drawing to a close, the German army was closing in on Moscow, just a few miles from occupying the Russian capital. In fact, it was reported that the German soldiers could see the spires of the Kremlin and were on the verge of taking the Soviet Union out of the war with one final push.

Before the war started between Germany and the Soviet Union, Japan had invaded Siberia with a large army and was only beaten back by a million man Soviet army sent to Siberia by Stalin. By the time the war with Germany started, the Japanese and Soviet armies were faced off in Siberia, neither moving, but both suspicious of the other. Stalin needed these men in Moscow to fight the Germans, but he also felt that they needed to remain in Siberia to protect it from Japan, with which they were not yet at war.

Back in Tokyo, the Soviet spy went to dinner one night at a restaurant favored by Japanese generals. While he was eating, several high ranking generals came in for dinner and sat at a table near him. Unbeknown to them, the spy spoke fluent Japanese and understood everything the generals said. Thinking that the "Caucasian" man next to them did not understand their language, they carelessly talked about their new plans to transfer all their troops now stationed in Mongolia facing the Soviet army in Siberia, south to French Indochina in preparation for the war against the United States.

The spy finished his dinner and immediately went to the Japanese equivalent of a Western Union office and sent a coded message to Stalin telling him of the Japanese plans. Stalin quickly ordered all of his Siberian troops back to Moscow on the Trans-Siberian railroad. The troops arrived in Moscow just in time to hit the tired, cold and hungry German troops so hard that they began a massive retreat away from Moscow which they never again threatened.

It is hard to know the effect the rescue of Moscow had on the outcome of the war. One can compare it to the defeat of the Russians in WW I when they surrendered and backed out of the war. If Moscow had fallen to the Germans would the Soviet Union have surrendered to Germany in 1941? Who knows?

It is firmly believed by historians that the German retreat from Moscow was a major turning point in WW II, and it was all caused by a Russian spy in Tokyo named Richard Sorge whose life, it is reported, was the inspiration for the James Bond stories. He was handsome, an alcoholic and famous womanizer who had lived in Japan for many years, but a man who had a significant effect on the outcome of the war. It would be interesting to know more about his life. He was later executed by the Japanese for being a spy.

The Soviet T-34 Tank – Battle at Kursk, Belarus

The Germans had the best tank in the war until the Soviets introduced their new T-34 medium tank. It was introduced to the world in the greatest tank battle in WW II on the plains outside of Kursk, Belarus. The Germans were aware that their enemy had developed and were building a new medium tank, but they were not concerned that it would be a match for their Tiger and Panther heavy tanks. In 1941 the Wehrmacht planned a massive tank attack against Kursk in Belarus as their kick off drive back to Moscow. None of the Allies had a tank to match the Germans, although the T-34 had not yet been proven in battle.

The Soviet army had deployed over a hundred new T-34 tanks in the forest outside of Kursk as they waited for the German heavy tanks that were headed toward them across the plains. The German soldiers were confident of their tanks as they headed east toward the city.

As they approached the forest outside of Kursk, the German troops suddenly heard the sound of many dozen tank engines start up. Within a few seconds, with their guns blazing, dozens of brand new T-34 Soviet tanks burst out of the forest headed full speed at the German Panzers. It was the largest ever massive tank battle, and the T-34's drove the German Panzers away from Kursk. It was the second time that the Wehrmacht had been turned away from Moscow, and they would never be that close again. The march was now on to Berlin, led by the T-34 medium tank.

The T-34 was fast, heavily armored with a long barrel 76 mm gun and thick armored plating on its turret and front end. The Soviet army lost hundreds of the tanks before the war was over, but they proved to be very effective in fighting the larger and heavier German tanks. The German tanks were difficult to repair and stayed out of action for long periods of time when damaged. The T-34 turned the tide of Germany's advance into the Soviet Union and had a significant effect on the outcome of the war in the east.

Miscellaneous

There were other Allied inventions and developments during the war that were instrumental in our victory. England invented radar, and the United States perfected it to the point that it was instrumental in our navy's fire control. We sank many Japanese ships at night when they couldn't be seen because of radar. Both Germany and Japan eventually developed radar later in the war.

Of great importance was the breaking of the German secret code (Enigma) by Great Britain, the American breaking of the Japanese diplomatic code in 1941and its navy code (JN-25) in 1942 as mentioned in earlier chapters. All three of these accomplishments were extremely important, but each requires a book of its own to cover properly. The U.S. Navy eventually developed sonar and associated techniques that allowed them to eliminate the German submarine threat in the Atlantic. By the end of 1944, the German submarine force had the highest rate of casualties of any unit on either side during the war. There are many other less significant but equally important inventions that all contributed to our ultimate victory that will not be covered here.

CHAPTER SEVENTEEN

War is Hell So, Don't Do It Haphazardly

"War is hell" as General Sherman said in 1864. But there has been no World War III and there probably won't be, at least not against Germany or Japan. It can be argued that the dropping of the atomic bombs has created a condition called MAD, mutual assured destruction, that keeps the major powers at peace overcoming the advantages of a large army.

It has been estimated that Russia now has over fifteen thousand nuclear warheads. The good news is that because of MAD, they have not launched one against anyone, nor have we. There have been several close calls, the Cuban Missile Crisis for one. But the sabers have stayed in their scabbards and humanity is muddling on from one crisis to another. We can only hope that we will never be caught unprepared against attack again nor will we use our strength unwisely.

There are many lessons available from World War II, but have we learned them? Let's list a few:

- Never underestimate your enemy.
- Never overestimate your enemy.
- Identify your enemy's intentions.
- Identify your enemy's strengths and weaknesses.
- Maintain a modern intelligent network including spies

on the ground and surveillance satellites in the sky.
- Sometimes your intelligence network tells you things you don't want to hear. Too bad.
- Modernize your fighting forces.
- Identify your specific goals early and be prepared to alter them if the situation changes.
- Prepare for the war you are going to fight not the one you want to fight.
- Maintain the ability to develop and build your own weapons.
- It is not necessary to keep a large standing army during peacetime.
- Just because a potential enemy has weapons of mass destruction doesn't mean that he will use them. But he might.
- Be prepared to mobilize at a moment's notice.
- Build just enough weapons to scare your potential enemies during peacetime.
- Don't rely on the last war's weapons or tactics.
- Presume that overseas bases and ships will be attacked.
- Negotiations are better than war.
- Never start nor continue a war without your public's support.
- Be prepared to compromise but don't give up your basic principles.
- Don't push around smaller countries just because you can.
- Spread the war effort evenly among your people.
- Don't let prejudice blind your judgment of other nations or cultures.
- Most wars are fought for economic, not political, reasons.
- Don't make promises to your public that you can't keep.

- You don't have to win every battle to win a war.
- A potential enemy is not likely to announce his intentions in advance.
- Don't lie to your public. They will eventually catch on and then they will not trust you again.
- Help your enemies to recover once you have beaten them. Don't let religious or racial prejudices cloud your view of your enemy's skills or capabilities.

So, there you have it, lessons from World War II, best learned from our, and our enemy's mistakes. Have we learned any of them? It often does not seem like it, and we may not be as lucky next time. Neither the conflict in Vietnam nor the invasions of Iraq, Syria or Afghanistan shows that we have learned anything.

We have listed some of the good things and bad things in WW II. Had any of them turned out differently, the war might have been lost, or at least prolonged for several more years. We civilians were not aware of most of them which is probably a good thing. We had enough to worry about as it was.

Last Thoughts

Might we have lost the war if things had been done differently? That depends on which way things might have gone. Let's look at each one:

The Axis had not made so many mistakes:

The war would definitely have dragged on for several years longer than it did and many more Americans would have been killed. Maybe we would have grown tired of the slaughter and sewed for a negotiated peace. We would still have had the atomic bomb so that may have insured eventual victory.

Japan bombed the West Coast and the fuel storage tanks at Pearl Harbor and ignored our Pacific Fleet.

With no war making capability on the West Coast, it would have been impossible to counter Japan's aggression in the Pacific. By the time we could have rebuilt our war making industries, Japan would have concurred all of South-east Asia. We would have sewed for peace without winning the war.

If Japan's navy had steamed directly for Southeast Asia and by-passed Pearl Harbor.

What's this got to do with us? This would be the isolationist motto and we would never get involved. Japan would rule the world and we would be a second class nation.

Fortunately Japan did the one thing that "awoke the sleeping giant," and attacking Pearl Harbor caused their defeat and insured America's dominance in the world for many years to come.

www.ingramcontent.com/pod-product-compliance
Lightning Source LLC
Chambersburg PA
CBHW021652120626
46545CB00002B/819

*9 7 9 8 8 8 6 1 5 2 5 6 2 *